MOVIES IN CLOSE-UP

Getting the Most from Film & Video

- LOVE - SCI-FI
- WAR - HEROES
- & MORE

Alan MacDonald

INTERVARSITY PRESS
DOWNERS GROVE, ILLINOIS 60515

Published in the United States of America by InterVarsity Press, Downers Grove, Illinois, with permission from Universities and Colleges Christian Fellowship, Leicester, England. Published in England as Films in Close-Up.

InterVarsity Press is the book-publishing division of InterVarsity Christian Fellowship, a student movement active on campus at hundreds of universities, colleges and schools of nursing in the United States of America, and a member movement of the International Fellowship of Evangelical Students. For information about local and regional activities, write Public Relations Dept., InterVarsity Christian Fellowship, 6400 Schroeder Rd., P.O. Box 7895, Madison, WI 53707-7895.

ISBN 0-8308-1313-6

Printed in the United States of America ∞

Library of Congress Cataloging-in-Publication Data
MacDonald, Alan, 1958-
   Movies in close-up: getting the most from film and video/Alan
MacDonald.
     p.   cm.
   Includes index.
   ISBN 0-8308-1313-6
   1. Motion pictures—Moral and ethical aspects. 2. Motion
pictures—Religious aspects—Christianity. 3. Motion pictures—
Reviews.   I. Title.
PN1995.5.M236
791.43'75—dc20
92-269
CIP

15	14	13	12	11	10	9	8	7	6	5	4	3	2	1
04	03	02	01	00	99	98	97	96	95	94	93	92		

To my parents,
who put up with a film critic
in their house for many years.

Poltergeist
Ghostbusters

1

UNDER THE INFLUENCE

PERSUASIVE PICTURES?

> **"Mickey is universal. He's just as popular in Moscow and Leningrad—these places where he's never been, there's all these rip-offs in copyright terms all over the world. He's on every t-shirt in the world—I saw him in the wilds of New Guinea five years ago."**[1]

Who are we talking about here? A politician? A revolutionary? A legendary writer? No. Mickey Mouse of course—the first cartoon film star. A moon-faced sixty-year-old mouse with oversized black ears and a voice that never broke. There are few people—adult or child—in the 1990s who wouldn't instantly recognize him.

Film, compared with the other arts, is still just out of diapers. But its influence belies its age. You only have to look at the popularity enjoyed by the stars it has produced. Even in the silent era Charlie Chaplin could claim, "I am known

in parts of the world by people who have never heard of
Jesus Christ."[2] During the 1914-18 war effort it was the film
stars—Chaplin, Pickford and Fairbanks—that they turned
to to raise money and morale.

The influence of films today can be seen in an industry
that goes far beyond the release of a single picture. When the
blockbuster *Batman* finally reached our screens in 1989, Bat-
mania seemed to have swept the country. The Batman logo
was everywhere in shops, newspapers, mugs and on T-shirts
worn by children too young to remember the original Marvel
Comics caped-crusader. A similar hype-wave can be remembered when *E.T.* was released (at $376 million still the big-
gest-grossing film of all time). E.T.'s catchphrase "Phone
home" almost claimed its own place in the English language.

Popular Art
Other arts such as music and literature are hugely influenced
by the success of film. Movie-theme tunes such as "Ghostbusters" can leap straight to chart-topping status; books
such as *A Room with a View* or *A Passage to India* are suddenly read by people who had never previously heard of
E. M. Forster.

All this is quite remarkable when you consider that many
had predicted the death of cinema within our lifetime. The
coming of the video revolution was expected to sweep it
away. But far from undercutting audience figures, video
seems to have swelled the queues at the box office. In 1987
nearly twenty-four million people were going to the cinema
in America *every week,* plus a further one and a half million
in the UK. This represents a steady rise in audiences since
1980. Where once the story was of cinemas closing down,

now new multi-screen complexes are opening up. In Britain, where the multiplex is relatively new, they already account for a quarter of audiences. Meanwhile the home-video market is growing so fast that it is always outstripping money made at the box office. In 1987 video sales and rentals brought in $7.5 billion in the USA alone.

Who's Watching?

"Who are the people flocking to the cinemas and video shops?" Films are generally seen as entertainment for the young market. There is strong evidence to support this be- lief—70% of cinema-goers in the UK are under twenty-five, and the percentage is higher in America. More than half of video rentals are to teenagers. The teen market doesn't ac- count for all cinema audiences however. The blockbuster "family films" of the 70s and 80s also had one eye on wooing parents back to the cinema. More recently a wave of "thirty- something" films *(When Harry Met Sally; Parenthood; Sex, Lies and Videotape;* etc.) suggests that cinema is holding on to the generation that grew up with the Beatles. Above all, popular film (unlike theater, opera, classical music and dance) is cheap, classless, mass entertainment. Its enthusi- asts include everyone from young children still hooked on the latest Disney character to lecturers in film study majoring on the political cinema of South America.

Film reaches the parts of us that other arts don't reach. It can combine the excitement of a rock soundtrack with the twists and turns in plot of a paperback thriller. It offers the visual magic of television but (at the cinema) on a bigger, brighter, more spectacular scale. Nothing can touch the spec- tacle of cinema—when Indiana Jones is chased by a gigantic boulder we feel it is bearing down on *us* in the audience. Today, multimillion-dollar budgets are spent on locations, lavish costumes and special effects. The sum total can be an all-out assault on the senses that is irresistible.

Fan or Critic?

What's the purpose of this book on film and video then? Is it a fan book or a film critic's book? Both. At the outset I should confess that I love watching films and will watch as many as I can in a year. I enjoyed *Dick Tracy* as well as *Babette's Feast, The Last Emperor* as well as *Who Killed Roger Rabbit?* This book concentrates on popular mainstream cinema. While it is a shame to miss out on lesser-known gems like *Jean de Florette,* I don't subscribe to the view that art-house films with English subtitles are better by definition. And by narrowing our focus to the big films of recent years there is obviously a better chance that the reader will have seen the films in question.

One reason for writing this book is to pass on my enthusiasm for films. If reading about some of the films reviewed in this book makes you want to see them—for the first or the fifteenth time—I shall feel it's been worthwhile.

But there is a second purpose behind this book. Ten years ago I studied the history of film—everything from the silent comedy of the Keystone Kops to the "heavy" European directors like Bergman and Fellini. At the end of three years of scribbling notes in the semi-darkness, I discovered that watching films, discussing and writing about them had helped me to see more in them. I noticed things that I hadn't seen there before. The way themes kept cropping up in the subtext of a film, the way color and visual images were used.

I realized that every film has its own message, be it as simple as "the tough guys win" message of *Rambo, Rocky, Lethal Weapon* and company.

So the second purpose then is to try and take a closer look at some of the messages that are coming across in the big films of our generation. Films are often seen as harmless entertainment, a couple of hours of escapism from the daily grind of life. But this assumes that we leave our minds and emotions outside the cinema door. When we watch a film, how does it influence us on a subconscious level? Do the role models, solutions and arguments in a film affect the way we think and behave when we go back home?

Mirrors or Persuaders?

The question could be summarized as, "Are films mirrors or persuaders?" Do they simply hold up a mirror to society, showing us what we are like in the late twentieth century, or are films subtly persuasive, offering us dreams to aspire to and even morals to live by?

It's a chicken-or-egg-type question. Do films copy us or do we copy films? Evidence can be found to support both views. On one hand, the film industry rarely misses a chance to cash in on trends that are already around—remember punk movies, dance movies, yuppie movies and baby-boom movies? On the other hand, film has often been held responsible for starting trends. There was the pumping-iron craze launched by a thousand would-be Arnold Schwarzeneggers or the fashion for khakis and bush hats first modelled in films like *Out of Africa*.

None of these examples is particularly conclusive, and there are few statistics which shed any light on the question.

Perhaps we need to start by asking how we watch films and whether we are likely to be affected by them as a result.

Movie Dreaming

It has been said that we glance at TV but gaze at films. A group of people watching television may talk, make cups of coffee, or even leave the room entirely while the program is still in progress. TV can be like the background "muzak" in restaurants. The exact opposite is true in the cinema—all our attention is focused on the screen images in front of us. We go to the movies to watch—and if someone in the row behind talks through the entire picture we are liable to push their ice cream into their face.

John Ellis has argued the similarities between watching films and dreaming.[3] We enter a darkened room and recline in comfort, avoiding all activities except watching and listening. As in dreams, we receive images in an intensified state and suspend our normal judgments. If Superman flies through space or a car travels through time *(Back to the Future)* we accept the fact without question. We don't expect the plausibility of real life.

At the same time as suspending normal judgments we can identify strongly with elements in the film. And, just as in dreams, we don't limit ourselves to identifying only with the hero or heroine. Our personalities are a mixture of complex tendencies, and in one film we may identify at different points with the lover, killer, victim, protector, male or female. It is something like seeing all the contradictory impulses of our personality passing before us in colorful procession. To say that "we identified" with one particular character underestimates the range of emotions we pass through in a film.

While we are in this state of dream-like consciousness, film reaches us through a unique combination of story, sound and visual energy to provide a total experience that is brighter, louder and larger than life itself. Critics refer to the magic of the movies probably because magic is the best way we can describe the experience of two hours in the dark watching moving images of light that dwarf us in size.

Dissecting Dreams

So we respond to films partly on an imaginative and subconscious level. We talk about being "caught up" in a film, "totally involved" or "on the edge of our seats." Even the language we use suggests that emotional involvement is a crucial part. Of course, if it's only "pure entertainment" or "harmless escapism" it matters little how involved we become. Films have nothing to do with reality, nothing to say about our own lives. But don't they?

Take even the most escapist fantasy film, like the original *Back to the Future*. For all the "play it for laughs" story line and characters, aren't there real questions we identify with in the film? For instance, "Are we saddled with the past and the failures of our parents? Does our background determine the future, or can we make our own choices?" These are questions connected with our own lives and are at the heart of the film's popularity as much as the thrills, special effects or the comedy.

Films deal with real questions, but they cannot convey a balanced discussion of both sides of an argument, as in a televised debate. Film is committed. It relies on dramatic form and immediate impact. It reaches conclusions and sometimes justifies them by the sympathy we feel for the characters involved. The danger, of course, is that we're persuaded that an action is right simply because we see it from the point of view of one character. It's hard to argue with Rambo when he brandishes a machine gun as the solution to the world's problems. Our heads may say he's wrong but our hearts may be too involved in the drama of the fight for survival. Similarly, in a love story we can find ourselves willing the husband to cheat on his boring wife and leap into bed with the desirable other woman. The dice has been loaded.

Under the Guard
Films have a habit of slipping under the guard of our convictions and taking possession of our emotional sympathies. In suspending our normal judgments about what is plausible we can also jettison our beliefs about what is right and wrong. At the end of the day we might say, "It was only a film," but is it possible that an experience that sometimes moves us to anger, triumph, tears or laughter does not take any root in our subconscious attitudes?

To take an obvious example, if we watch countless films of the "psycho-slasher" variety, where the camera tracks the female victims from the murderer's viewpoint, won't our view of women be degraded as a result? The pictures tell us women are dumb helpless victims while implying that aggressive male sexuality is fun. Watching will reinforce negative stereotypes of women and even encourage the idea that male violence is really okay. It may be claiming too much to say that these films can turn men into rapists but it's also naive to argue that they are harmless. Rape and assault are becoming commonplace in our society today, and Hollywood does women no favors by giving these crimes peep-show status.

This is to dwell on the darker aspects of cinema. The vast majority of films are about more savory subjects and have a lot to offer in terms of a positive influence. While some Christians believe it is safer to avoid film and videos altogether, most would accept that films can entertain, inform and even teach us new truths about life. To list some examples, most Christians would accept that a film like *Chariots of Fire* did a lot for the image of Christianity as a living, vibrant faith. Films like *The Mission* have also brought religious belief under the spotlight and dealt with important moral dilemmas.

Other films can also be applauded for their stand against injustice and inhumanity. *Cry Freedom* and *Mississippi Burning* in their different ways are both powerful protests against the cancerous growth of racism.

Films included in this book deal with war, relationships, history and outer space. There is much that is true in them, much that can be admired in the crafts of acting, directing and technical achievement, and much that can be a positive influence.

The million-dollar question is, "How do we distinguish what is positive from what is questionable or negative?" Do we have to swallow every film whole, or can we enjoy the best dishes while leaving certain bits on the side of the plate?

Films in This Book

To answer the last question it would be possible to look at the language of film in a theoretical way. You'll probably be relieved to know that this isn't the approach taken in this book. Instead I have selected around twenty-five of the most successful films of recent years as examples of their kind.

They are arranged according to category—war films, space films, horror films, romantic films, etc. Naturally these categories have their limitations, but it will be useful to compare films of a similar kind alongside each other.

Although the acting, music or technical quality of a film may be commented on in passing, the main focus will be on *what the film is saying.* In each chapter this will mean asking certain key questions.

To take an example, in the chapter about war films we'll ask, "What is a human being according to the films? Are we machines, animals or moral beings? And if morality exists, how do we decide what is right or wrong?"

Few of us watching *Platoon* or *The Killing Fields* will know what war is like at firsthand, but the films can nevertheless have a strong impact on us. We identify with the characters even if the situation is beyond our experience. This is because the choices they face are still familiar to us— loyalty to friends or looking after number one, bullying the weak or risking our reputation to protect them. The characters make decisions in the context of extraordinary, maybe life-or-death situations, but they are still related to the decisions we all face in our lives. Seeing these choices dramatized on the big screen acts out solutions for us. But as Christians, we need to ask whether these are the solutions of the Bible or Hollywood.

Intelligent Life?
"Most of the films in Hollywood are made for half-wits and certainly not for intelligent people."[4] That was actor James Mason's verdict in his day, and any book about cinema today is still up against the prejudice that films are not subjects

worthy of serious discussion. Critical evaluation of books has long been part of our education system, and media studies are now getting a toehold, but films are still widely regarded as popular entertainment that can safely be ignored. In this way cinema and video are left unhindered to spread their influence among a growing audience of eight- to thirty-something-year-olds.

Occasionally the sex-and-violence issue flares up again, and the censors go into a new juggling act with the ratings system to keep people quiet. But little attention is paid to what films are actually saying. Is it more important that someone took their clothes off in a film or that the film is suggesting that it is okay to use each other like sexual commodities? Too often it's the nudity that gets noticed while the wider issue is ignored.

In a culture where the written word is increasingly the province of the few and verbal debate has virtually been reduced to a maximum of three minutes, what has replaced the word is the picture. This book is written in the belief that we ignore the influence of films and videos at our peril.

2
TO BOLDLY GO

There is a story that during the production of *E.T.,* Melissa Mathison, its writer, discovered many similarities between her screenplay and events in the life of Christ. Mathison, educated in a Catholic convent in Hollywood, went to the director, Steven Spielberg, and told him what she'd found. "I'm Jewish and I don't want to hear anything about this," was Spielberg's reaction.[1]

Mathison's discovery should not have been surprising. Parallels have often been found between science fiction and religion. Science fiction asks the question whether there may be more to reality than the material world. Christianity in answer points to the heavens, the existence of a Creator and life beyond this earth.

You have only to sit through five minutes of one of the space classics of recent cinema to see how closely the language and imagery of the two are entwined. Science has been the dominant force of our age—at one point it was believed technology held the solution to all problems. But it has still not found an answer to humanity's sense of loneliness in the universe and our desire for meaning. This is where the "fiction" part of "science fiction" comes into play. It satisfies the yearning for other worlds and other beings, rich in the symbolism of religion. It is no coincidence that when UFOs appear in films they are always bathed in majestic and mysterious light. These are beings descending from the heavens whom we look to for the redemption or judgment of the human race.

This chapter focuses on some of the parallels between space fantasy films and the Christian world view. There is enough material available in this area alone for one author to have devoted a whole book to the subject.[2] Here we'll want to probe a little deeper than just playing a "spot the similarity" game. If the films identify godlike powers behind the universe, what are they like and what do they have to tell us about the purpose of life on planet Earth?

Close Encounters of the Third Kind (1977)

Close Encounters was in many ways a watershed in modern sci-fi. Space films were not thought bankable products at the time, and only Stanley Kubrick's *2001* had really caught the imagination of cinema audiences.

Close Encounters opens with an old man relating a story about the sun coming up, which is relayed to us via subtitles. Unexplained scenes in shifting international locations keep cutting into the scenes of ordinary life of two families in Indiana. An air-traffic control tower receives a UFO sighting while a child sees toy trucks and cars zooming around the room at night. Jack Kroll compares the opening with *2001,* "Kubrick's image was apocalyptic, magnificently pretentious. Spielberg's is also full of portent, but it's friendly, domestic and touchingly whimsical."[3]

While the investigative team of scientists are following clues around the globe, Roy and Jillian are receiving messages from outer space. The story of the film is that of everyman and everywoman trying to keep a rendezvous with mysterious beings from another planet. Spielberg sets up an immediate contrast between the professionals (the scientists) and the children.

The children are accepting and curious about the mysterious happenings, but the adults are often skeptical. As a result only the adults are scared in this film.

Childlike Faith

Roy qualifies to meet the aliens by demonstrating childlike qualities, sculpting his mashed potato into the form of Devil's Tower—the rendezvous site. His wife sides with the adults by leaving him. On the verge of breakdown, Roy stares out of the window, isolated from his neighbors carrying on their middle-class rituals of lighting barbecues and mowing lawns. Roy and Jillian's isolation is due to a form of spiritual awakening where they begin to share the imagination and openness that children show the visitors to their earth. The authorities surround the area with barriers just as the neighbors hide behind barriers of commonplace rituals. Spielberg's theme is repeated in many of his films—adults need to become children again to experience the wonder and mystery of the universe. If the idea seems familiar it's possibly because it's so close to Jesus' words about faith, "I tell you the truth, unless you change and become like little children, you will never enter the kingdom of heaven" (Matthew 18:3). In *Close Encounters* only those who have this sort of faith will meet the aliens.

Roy gets his chance to enter the kingdom of space at the end of the film when he boards the UFO. The aliens themselves emerge from the spacecraft in shafts of warm, bright backlighting that lends a heavenly appearance. They walk in a childlike way—one design proposal was for headpieces similar to a fetus. Many critics were disappointed with the final scene where we see the face of one adult E.T. But, "there is a reason for showing the alien's face. . . . The film subverts the familiar paranoia of science fiction made during the Cold War. The alien must be seen in order to banish fear."[4] This represents Spielberg's major innovation from the 50s sci-fi's he grew up with—the visitors from another world are not threatening but friendly. Spielberg supposes a benign presence beyond the stars and one which needs human faith, curiosity and adventure to enter into a relationship. No real clues are given about the nature of these otherworldly beings. *Close Encounters* leaves this to other films. Its contribution is to identify the enemy of faith as the obstinate adult tendency to hide behind barriers of fear and skepticism.

E.T. (1982)

In 1982 a squat, wrinkled, mud-colored alien with a perpetual chest cold became a media sensation, appearing on everything from bedspreads to the cover of *Rolling Stone* magazine. *E.T.*, the space fantasy with a sweet center, went on to be the biggest box-office earner of all time.

The film in many ways takes up where *Close Encounters* left off. When the palace of lights that is the alien spacecraft takes off, Spielberg revives the familiar Disney tradition of "What happens if the little guy misses the bus home?" In this case what happens is that the alien walks into the life of Elliot—a shy, lonely boy in desperate need of a friend.

Unusual for Spielberg, the film has relationships at its heart. Elliot is as stranded and alone on earth as E.T. His father has left home, his working mother is too busy to notice him and his brother and sister are either too old or too young to be his friend. When Elliot upsets his mother, the elder brother demands, "Why don't you grow up and think of how other people feel for a change?" It is no coincidence that, through E.T., Elliot learns to literally *feel* for someone else. The relationship between the boy and the alien is symbiotic in a way that is never explained. When E.T. sees John Wayne and Maureen O'Sullivan kiss on the television, Elliot kisses the prettiest girl in the class. The film doesn't suggest the alien is controlling the boy but that there is an almost spiritual sympathy between them. If E.T. is seen as a type of Christ, as Mathison and others have argued, then the belief that Christ lives through his followers is the parallel here. In an echo of Christ's parting promise, "I am with you always, to the very end of the age" (Matthew 28:20), E.T. points to Elliot's heart and says, "I'll be right here."

More importantly, the quality E.T. comes to teach is essentially love. The alien has a heart that glows when he is afraid or warmly touched. In the opening scenes Elliot is only able to express resentment about his missing father, but it's clear he has discovered other emotions by the end. When E.T. lies apparently dead, Elliot tells him, "I don't know how to feel any more, I love you," which mysteriously seems to revive the alien's heart. Naturally, since this is a Hollywood film about children, the nature of love is explored mainly at the senti-mental level associated with Disney animal movies. Neverthe-less *E.T.*'s unique appeal to adults and children alike can only be explained by an instinctive response to a quality of love rarely seen in films and supremely found in the life of Jesus.

Science is, as ever, both the enemy and the door to wonder and belief in the Spielberg framework. In one of the film's visual jokes, science appears at the door as a spaceman in a white suit come to take the extra-terrestrial away. But all the paraphernalia of modern medicine fails to keep E.T. alive where Elliot's appeal to love succeeds. On the other hand, Spielberg cannot resist a fascination with the magic of the modern material world. Pizzas, toys, dolls, train sets and cal-culators assume a life of their own in his films. The theolo-gian Jung has suggested that "modern man appropriates ma-chine images to his own magical purposes, and turns the stuff of science to myth and religion."[5] This is true of Spiel-berg more than any other contemporary director. He seems to suggest that science is only an enemy when it tries to form the universe into straight lines and cannot admit to the un-expected and even supernatural.

Dealing with the Divine

What are we to make of the often quoted parallels to Christ in the film? Al Millar in his pamphlet "E.T. You're more than a movie star," lists at least thirty-three parallels. A few will serve to illustrate here:

☐ E.T. had a prior extra-terrestrial existence.

☐ His early life was submerged or hidden.

☐ He came to little children.

☐ He suffers a death and resurrection.

☐ He finally ascends to his original home.

Other commentators are not impressed. Tom O'Brien compares it to both *2001* and *Superman*, "According to their plots, whatever comes out of a spaceship must either save or destroy us." In this respect he argues Spielberg's vision is spiritually defective. "As a myth maker he shares the defects of other creators of sci-fi, not excess but defect of imagination. Their substitute religion is based on an unspiritual premise: that something physical is going to save or destroy us, depending on whether the E.T.'s involved are angelic or satanic."[6]

O'Brien's argument carries weight if we take space fantasies at face value. Sci-fi, however, can also be taken on an allegorical or parable level (witness C. S. Lewis's space trilogy), and in this light a visitor from another planet could be seen as merely Christ-like. E.T. is a physical character with physical characteristics but so was Christ. The parallels between the two are so numerous that they are difficult to ignore. This was probably not Mathison's (and certainly not Spielberg's) intention but the coincidence points to the way the age-old themes of love, death, resurrection and spiritual re-birth will surface whenever a savior character like E.T. is created.

Of course, too much should not be read into the parallels. E.T. has limitations as a savior figure. His death does not have the atoning significance which is central to Christ's death on the cross. The soft-hearted alien ultimately belongs to the cupboard world of cuddly toys and the stories of Peter Pan that Elliot's mother reads to his sister. Spielberg's story is more magical than spiritual, but in its appeal to unconditional love succeeds on a spiritual level. As Robert Short comments, "E.T. speaks to us because it's an embrace like his that all of us want and need. In E.T.'s love we see a love very much like the love that can be seen in Christ—especially in the crucified Christ. For those arms of Christ stretched open on the cross represent the widest possible embrace ... an embrace encompassing the whole world."[7]

Star Trek (1979-1988)

A shot of a spaceship pulls out to show the immensity of the galaxy surrounding it. "Space—the final frontier," intones a disembodied voice. "These are the voyages of the Starship Enterprise ... to explore strange new worlds, to boldly go where no man has gone before."

Star Trek is the longest-running space fantasy ever created. The now familiar crew of the Enterprise has voyaged from the primitive special effects of early television on to five adventures on the big screen. Spock still raises one quizzical eyebrow, Scottie still grumbles from the engine room, "I'm not sure she can take any more, Cap'n!" and James T. Kirk is still at the helm. Here lies the secret of *Star Trek's* success. The stories may be predictable and the special effects not in the *Star Wars'* league, but we stay to watch the familiar characters in their latest life-or-death escapade.

The screenplays usually stick to the tried-and-trusted formula of foiling the evil genius who wants to take over the universe. In *Star Trek 1* and *3* the alien Hell's Angels—the Klingons—are the enemy. In *Star Trek 2* the wrath of Khan threatens the solar system. In other films Kirk and crew save the whale *(3)* and even search for God *(5)*. A typical blend of the space thriller and pseudo-mysticism is found in

Star Trek 3: The Search for Spock—arguably the best of the films.

In this scenario Spock's dead body has been left on Genesis—an experimental planet. Spock's dad turns up demanding his Catra (soul in Vulcan-speak) to be brought to the planet Vulcan. When Kirk returns to the planet Genesis he finds it is aging at high speed and, just to complicate matters, the Klingons turn up, seeking the secret of the Genesis effect.

Star Trek plots always sound as ridiculous as this when you try to explain them, and the adventures are played out with an enjoyable line in tongue-in-cheek humor. When Lt. O'Hara tells a young officer, "This isn't reality; it's fantasy," she is reciting the Trekkie code that anything goes, as long as the actors can get away with it.

The Genesis Effect

Yet amid all the fast-paced comedy, *Star Trek* has a weakness for mysticism in which religious parallels frequently surface. When Spock's coffin is found on Genesis, the body is missing. He has apparently been "regenerated by the Genesis effect." The planet itself is the work of an experiment to make a dead moon into "a living, breathing planet capable of sustaining whatever life-forms we see fit." But as usual human beings prove a flawed creator. Kirk's son, David, has used "proto-matter" in the project and so brought a curse on nature so that Genesis becomes a paradise lost. David not only takes the role of a biblical Adam but later of a redeemer too. When he is killed by a Klingon it is reported that "he gave his life to save us."

The final scene, where Spock is returned to the planet Vulcan, is awash with quasi-religious ritual. Mystical music plays, a gong is beaten, Spock is carried by handmaidens in diaphanous gowns, and an old priestess addresses Bones, "McCoy, son of David, since thou art human, we cannot expect thee to understand fully. . . ." With the aid of much similar mumbo-jumbo Spock's soul is returned by McCoy, who has been keeping it warm for him till he needed it.

As usual, Hollywood is happy to mix elements of Christian tradition with a spoonful of Eastern mysticism to raise one of its characters back to life. It is the ending of *Star Trek 3* that betrays that the films are really just plain old humanism dressed up in funny costume. "You came back for me; why would you do this?" asks Old Pointy Ears. "Because the needs of the one outweighed the needs of the many," replies Kirk. Spock is continually shown in the series that human emotion, which he rejects as illogical, is what separates human beings from the rest of the class. *Star Trek* elevates the human capacity for love, spontaneity, loyalty and sacrifice to an almost mystical level. The *Enterprise* may set out to explore strange new worlds and even find God, but it always winds up back with good old Captain Kirk and the wonder of the human race.

Star Wars/The Empire Strikes Back/Return of the Jedi (1977, 1980, 1983)

A long time ago in a distant galaxy a man called George Lucas remembered the action-packed Saturday matinees he used to watch as a boy and decided to attempt something similar for a new, more sophisticated generation. Thus was born the *Star Wars* trilogy which changed the face of the film industry overnight; sending the whole of Hollywood scrambling in search of the big blockbuster and relegating old favorites like the Western to the back of the shelf.

Ironically, Lucas's trilogy could fairly be described as a Western in space—the shoot-outs and chases are the same, it's just that bullets have been replaced by laser beams and horses by amazingly convincing model spaceships. Lucas, who describes himself as a religious person ("I believe in God and I believe in good"), attaches greater significance to the films. He sees them as "a psychological tool that children can use to understand the world better and their place in it. . . . It's very basic. It's where religion came from."[8]

The original *Star Wars* was released in 1977 and sets out the story of the good-guy rebels against the ruling powers of evil (the Empire). The major characters—Luke Skywalker, Darth Vader and friends are all introduced. The people are dwarfed by the stunning sets and spectacular effects, but Star Wars succeeds by creating its own mythology of the galaxy which can be traced through the three films as a continuing thread.

Good and Evil

Most striking is the film's portrayal of the conflict between good and evil. "May the force be with you," is the rallying cry against the storm troopers of the Empire. Many American church leaders welcomed the films at the time in terms of Christian allegory, and it's not difficult to see why.

Obi-Wan Kenobi could easily be taken as a Christ symbol. He is killed in battle with Darth Vader but returns from the dead in spiritual form to lead Luke in the ways of the Force. Hans Solo (note the name) is a type of modern man in his skepticism toward things supernatural—"Hocus-pocus religions and archaic weapons are no substitute for a good blaster at your side." Skywalker, on the other hand, is the believer-as-disciple who must learn to use the Force to defeat Vader and the powers of Evil. In *The Empire Strikes Back* Skywalker is sent to serve his apprenticeship under the instruction of Yoda, a Jedi master whose Spock ears denote wisdom. His instruction is couched in mystical terms:

YODA: A Jedi's strength flows from the Force. If once you step down the dark path . . consume you it will.

LUKE: Is the Dark side stronger?

YODA: No. . . . You will know the difference when you are calm, at peace.

A Jedi's powers are prophetic—he can glimpse the future—and, magically, he can lift objects by concentration. The source of the power, though, sometimes sounds closer to a mystical life-force than the power of God. Yoda tells us, "Life creates it, makes it grow. Its energy surrounds and binds us." If Yoda had been around to witness the spread of New Age philosophy one senses he could have become a leading guru.

The portrayal of evil in the trilogy is closer to the Christian framework. It is curious that the Devil has been discarded as a medieval superstition in modern Western society, yet he persistently appears in films wearing thin disguise. Darth Vader is a case in point. He was once a Jedi knight who has turned from the Light to serve the Dark side. Like the Devil he is a fallen angel and his motive, too, is power. Vader also plays the tempter to Skywalker—offering him a share in the Empire if he will join the Dark side. The battle between good and evil takes place within Luke's soul as the laser beams clash. The Force will finally win and this is where *Star Wars* most clearly shadows the Christian view. In the ultimate battle the final and total victory of the ultimate good has already been won (Colossians 2:15). The stories take place "a long time ago . . ."—we are living in a future secured by the fact that Evil has already been defeated once and for all.

The Fundamental Quest

Ultimately, any attempt to portray *Star Wars* as a Christian allegory will be flawed. The mythology it creates will at times satisfy the New Ager or the Buddhist as much as the Christian. With the exception of *E.T.*'s close parallels to the gospel stories, this is probably true of all the science fiction films reviewed here. Nevertheless, if the spiritual framework is often a ragbag of different beliefs, the fundamental quest of men and women within the space fantasy remains the same—to find a purpose and personality behind the universe.

The astronomer Carl Sagan has reached the same conclusion about UFO sightings: "The interest in UFOs and ancient astronauts seems at least partly the result of unfulfilled religious needs. The extraterrestrials are often described as wise, powerful, benign, human in appearance, and sometimes they are attired in long white robes. They are very much like gods or angels. . . . Indeed, a recent British survey suggests that more people believe in extraterrestrial visitations than in God."[9]

In the end our fantasies about space tell us more about ourselves than about the nature of the universe. Inside each of us a spiritual vacuum exists, a longing for a relationship that cannot be satisfied by anyone or anything on earth. Into this "God-shaped hole" we pour all our desires for what the perfect otherworld being should be. Interestingly, what we come up with (whether called E.T. or Obi-Wan) is often remarkably like Christ.

3
MY HERO— SO MACHO

At the beginning of the 90s there was a lot of talk about "the new man." Pictures of bare-chested men cradling sleeping infants have been featured in a glut of posters and advertisements. The new man changes diapers, he cooks and does his share of the housework, he's sensitive to the needs of his partner. As yet he hasn't made much of an impact in films, perhaps because Hollywood is skeptical that he exists (men and babies are still a subject for comedy, e.g., *Three Men and a Baby, Look Who's Talking*). It will be interesting to see if a new kind of hero or even heroine is born in the 90s, but for the moment we're stuck with what we've got.

Why do we need film heroes anyway? In box-office terms the answer is that they provide a face which is the selling point of the film. We go to see James Bond because we know what the character stands for. And it follows that what he does stand for must be something that a part of us secretly admires and aspires to. Screen heroes provide us with models for living. Even if we know the Bond lifestyle is remote from our own situation, it represents an image of how we'd like to live. On a simple level the desire to be like our heroes can be seen in copycat trends such as Rambo headbands and Indiana Jones hats.

Film heroes offer some concrete answers to some of the basic questions of life. What makes a complete human being? What are the qualities we should look for in ourselves? How should we go about solving our problems, and how should we relate to the opposite sex? In this chapter we'll look at some of cinema's answers to these questions.

Screen Heroes

The screen hero is less easy to define today than he would have been in the golden age of Hollywood. In the days of Fairbanks, Gable and Flynn a hero was recognized by his rugged good looks and his ability to fend off an army of villains while still finding time for a clinch with the heroine. A hero also followed a rigid code of honor which said that if the bad guy dropped his sword it had to be returned before he could be defeated in gentlemanly fashion.

This romantic ideal remained more or less intact until the late 50s and the rise of the anti-hero. Films like *Rebel Without a Cause, Room at the Top* and *Saturday Night and Sunday Morning* introduced a hero at odds with society who didn't mind playing dirty to get what he wanted. What then of the heroes of our own age? While everyone will have their own favorites, three screen heroes whose popularity has been proved by continual box-office success are James Bond, Indiana Jones and Rambo. It can be objected that these are all men. The sad truth is that women's status in popular film remains largely as the motivator for the exploits of the male hero.

Rambo (1982, 1985, 1988)

The simplest of the three heroes is undoubtedly John Rambo, inspiration for three *First Blood* films which rode the wave of success started by the *Rocky* films for Sylvester Stallone. The influence of the Rambo character can be judged by the fact that he spawned a whole generation of imitations in the blood, sweat and grunt school.

First Blood depicts a world which is a jungle and goes on to create a hero who is perfectly adapted to the law of the jungle. Stallone himself says, "I hope to establish a character that can represent a certain section of the American consciousness and through the entertainment be educational." If so, the educational lesson is, "Don't mess with Rambo, suckers!"

Most of the qualities the film pays tribute to are represented in Rambo's physique. The camera constantly dwells on a man built as a fighting machine. The muscles bulge on a body oiled with sweat, ugly scars hint at past battles and bullet belts crisscross the chest in readiness for the next. Rambo's face is set in a moody stare expressing a "make my day" challenge to anyone stupid enough to provoke him.

Focus on Pain

The second mark of Rambo's manhood is the ability to inflict and endure pain. Rambo's former colonel from Vietnam sums him up as "an expert in guerilla warfare, the best with guns, with knives, with his bare hands. Trained to ignore pain, ignore weather, to live off the land." *First Blood* continually reminds us of this status. Throughout the film, Rambo collects wounds like boys collect stamps. At one point a close-up dwells on blood seeping from a gash that Rambo sews up for himself as if pain were a word missing from his limited vocabulary.

Rambo is also a hero able to survive in primitive conditions. He can always fashion a spear and kill a wild pig if he gets hungry, and he carries a large hunting knife as a basic necessity of life. The pioneer spirit of the first settlers has always been held in high regard by Americans, and Rambo possesses their rugged, outdoor quality in abundance.

Focus on Authority

The final quality of the complete man, according to Rambo, is that he should have a healthy distrust for any authority. In the initial *First Blood* story a brush with a local sheriff leads to a full-scale manhunt in which Rambo attacks and mutilates half the state police force and national guard. This may seem excessive but the encore in part two is to wipe out most of an entire army when Rambo is double-crossed by the controllers of a government-backed mission.

Women, not surprisingly, play little part in Rambo films, unless they can handle a gun as well as a man. Neither does Rambo waste much time in discussing peaceful solutions, developing friendships or indulging in soul-searching. These are irrelevant qualities in the film's terms. Rambo's solutions to life's problems are refreshingly simple—knife it, shoot it or, even better, blow it up, which produces a more satisfying boom.

The justification for this has less to do with justice than pure revenge. "They drew first blood not me," says Rambo; little more excuse is apparently needed. The idea that revenge may not be a sufficient justification for killing or even that it should be left to God's judgment (Romans 12:19) is never at issue. *First Blood* films paint the enemy as people of no importance who deserve to die for being dumb enough to provoke the wrath of Rambo.

It is easy to dismiss Rambo and all the sequels as mindless fun for those with a taste for violence. But the popularity of the genre raises disturbing questions about the influence of heroes. Harvey Keitel comments, "We need heroes, they say and I agree. The question is, what kind of heroes? The hero that sprays the village with bullets and people topple over like cardboard figures experiencing no pain? We must depict the suffering and honor of that reality in order to grow a real hero. We don't need those heroes—those are lies!"[1]

The division between fantasy and reality blurs easily. Stallone himself writes the Rambo films, and much is made of the way he puts himself through gruelling survival courses in order to be in peak condition for the role. The myth created is that Stallone is Rambo. For the millions of teenagers who are his greatest followers the suspicion must be that violence is not only okay, it's the mark of a *real* man.

James Bond

If Rambo is characterized by the machine gun, James Bond is the man with the silencer-fitted pistol. The main ingredients of a Bond movie are clearly stated in the opening sequence where a naked woman usually appears floating or somersaulting over the silhouette of a gun. Bond's professional-assassin status and his sexual appeal go hand in hand. Bond films have been described as the longest-running male fantasy in existence. Now on his seventeenth sequel, Bond has survived by adapting to the changing times, retaining only a few of the hallmarks of Ian Fleming's original character.

The 60s Bond portrayed by Sean Connery was a professional who disposed of the KGB and got women into his bed with the same air of brute efficiency. Roger Moore's replacement of Connery was the substitution of the head prefect for the school bully. Timothy Dalton, the latest in the Bond mold, combines elements of both. He has the sophistication of Moore allied to the slightly wolfish appeal of Connery. Dalton's first film, *The Living Daylights* (1987), deserved the credit it got for restoring the thriller edge to the Bond film. The best Bond films (I would personally rule out the Moore era) keep the audience on the edge of their seats while playing the tongue-in-cheek note to perfection.

The essential ingredients of a Bond movie are by now well known. There must be a threat to global security that only James Bond can avert; the quest should take us to several exotic locations and introduce a number of new gadgets along the way. Bond will encounter a string of beautiful women and stage a final showdown with the evil genius who is intent on world domination. Ideally the film ends with spectacular explosions and the heroine in James's arms—until next time.

License to Kill

Like John Rambo, Bond provides us with certain clues to the make-up of a real man. Unlike Rambo, Bond belongs to the establishment; he works for the British civil service. However, he is never owned by his job. When another agent quotes official procedure at him Bond simply replies, "Stuff orders!" He is his own man. A common ground between all screen heroes is that they work in their own way, implying that successful people live by their own individual law, not by corporate decisions. It is up to us to decide what is right and wrong, we shouldn't depend on outside agencies.

Bond's agent number is 007, the double 0 signifying a license to kill. Again this is an essential ingredient of the male hero. Bond would never indulge in the wholesale carnage that is Rambo's stock in trade but without the gun and the expertise to use it, he would not be James Bond. The violence of a Bond film is justified by a sort of sleight of hand which depends on humor. Although we see real people killed, and often in gruesome ways, the sting is taken out by a quip that accompanies the death. Dalton sends an enemy plummeting to his death by removing the shoe he was holding on to. "He got the boot," James informs the heroine. Bond is the master of stylish assassination, always purging the offensiveness of the act with a joke.

Style is what sets Bond apart from the common crowd, whether he is killing a villain or choosing a champagne. He always knows the best vintage, always dresses for dinner and always knows which fork to use. It is as if the films assure us that it doesn't matter what we do, as long as we do it with style.

Perhaps the most worrying aspect of Bond's heroic makeup is his treatment of women. The opening sequence, mixing guns with the naked female image, suggests a disturbing element of sexual violence lurking beneath the surface. The

gun in cinema is often given phallic significance and Bond's
skill with it is equated with his sexual prowess. In *The Living
Daylights* a bikini-clad girl muses, "If only I could find a real
man," and Timothy Dalton promptly drops out of the sky
onto her boat. Dalton has just escaped from an opening sequence involving the death of three men which is the proof
of his manhood.

Bond Women

Women in the films are called "Bond girls" (a label as de-
meaning as nude pin-up girls). They are beautiful, scantily
dressed and magnetized by the British agent as easily as if
they were made of iron filings. Even minor female characters
such as chambermaids are driven to instantly offer themselves with innuendos like, "Is there anything I can do for
you?" Strong women only appear in Bond films as desirable
enemy agents who are only waiting for "a real man" to come
along so that they can return to being a sexual stereotype
themselves.

The Living Daylights represented a move away from the
traditional Bond image in concentrating romantic interest on
one girl (Maryon D'Abo) and omitting the bedroom scenes.
Whether this was due to the impact of the AIDS crisis in
1987 or the influence of feminism is hard to assess. What is
certain is that D'Abo's blonde cellist is still restricted to a
supporting role in the film. While she is allowed to develop
to the point where she commandeers a jeep and fights off
Russian soldiers, we are left in no doubt that she will always
be dependent on Bond's superior male powers.

In a climactic scene, Bond leaves her in charge of steering
the plane while he fights off the villain and defuses a bomb,

but he has to be back in time to rescue them from steering into a cliff face—just like a woman, she can't drive!

Mass slaughter is not James Bond's style, and there is no suggestion that killing should be relished in the Rambo vein. The glamor of the Bond film is perhaps more seductive in suggesting that real heroes kill when it's necessary and real men treat women as sexual objects because that is what women secretly desire.

Indiana Jones (1981, 1984, 1989)

In any poll of the most popular screen heroes of recent years Indiana Jones is likely to appear. The third in Steven Spielberg's "Boy's Own" adventure series, *Indiana Jones and the Last Crusade,* topped the UK box office receipts in 1989, showing the character has lost none of his appeal since he first arrived on the screen.

Both the plot and the hero of the Indiana saga owe a lot to the Saturday-matinee serials of the 30s and 40s. Spielberg collaborated with George Lucas *(Star Wars)* to create the movie equivalent of a ride at Disneyland—inexpensive, believable and action-packed. In this sense they are hugely enjoyable. Spielberg knows just how to run a roller-coaster; when to ease us up a slope with humor and suspense and when to swoop down into a hairpin bend at an impossible speed.

Indiana Jones is introduced as an archaeologist but is in reality an old-fashioned adventurer more at home in the Amazon jungle than the lecture theater. Of the three heroes considered here, Indie is probably the most human. Harrison Ford's character relies on his wit and resources to get him out of trouble, rather than an arsenal of weapons or gadgets.

He can suffer pain, show exhaustion and has a terror of snakes to emphasize his mortality. The Jones character doesn't have to be larger than life because the adventures themselves are on an epic scale.

Feet of Clay

The model for Indiana Jones was the white-hatted hero of the matinees. Spielberg, however, recognizes modern audiences demand different qualities in their hero. When Indie is first glimpsed in *Raiders of the Lost Ark* he emerges out of the shadows as a mysterious character—unshaven, shifty-eyed and clutching a bull-whip. It is almost as if Spielberg is deliberately subverting the old whiter-than-white image to suggest a modern hero must contain elements of "the bad guy" in his make-up to be credible.

Indie is a hero with feet of clay. When he fights he is capable of biting a villain's hand, kicking him in the crotch and throwing sand in his face. On one famous occasion a swordsman in black emerges from the crowd, only for Indie to shoot him with a revolver. (Spielberg admits Ford was suffering from a bad dose of diarrhea that day and this was the quickest way of wrapping up the scene.)[2] Spielberg is poking fun at the old romantic hero conventions. He's also suggesting that in the modern world a hero sometimes has to fight dirty to get what he wants. The rigid code of honor has been replaced by a pragmatism that gets results. Jones is always on the side of good against the evil of Nazism or black magic but the films do not portray him as a saint.

In his treatment of women Jones doesn't have the predatory instincts of James Bond but still belongs to the "treat 'em rough and tell 'em nothing" school of male heroes. In

Raiders Jones dismisses Marion's charge that he seduced her as a young girl with, "I did what I did." In *The Last Crusade* we discover Indie and his dad have both slept with the blonde German spy. Although this lands them in trouble, the suggestion is that our hero is just a chip off the old block. Unlike Bond, Indie confines himself to one woman at a time, but there is never any suggestion of a committed, lasting relationship. Indie, like most modern heroes, will appear with a new girl in tow in the next movie, implying that adventure in sexual relationships is as important as in archaeology.

As for heroines in the Indiana story they have to keep up with a gruelling pace of action but essentially remain in the role of helpless female needing to be rescued. Marion comes the nearest to breaking the mold—She's feisty, issues commands, swears, shoots guns, hits men, owns her own bar, drinks (and has drinking contests) and basically holds her own. But most of this behavior is in the first scene and establishes her spunky personality; much of the remaining film undercuts her behavior either verbally or visually.[3]

Identikit Heroes

Returning to our original questions about what sort of a model screen heroes provide for us, we can now build up something like an identikit picture. Firstly, a hero must be a man. He must be attractive to all women but attainable by none. He must be a man of action able to defend himself with guns, knives, whips and his bare hands. He should be prepared to kill when necessary. When faced with a problem he should trust to his personal instincts, taking orders from no one and certainly not worrying about divine beings unless they start zapping people with lightning (see *Raiders of the Lost Ark*).

This may be a simplified list drawn from a selective look at screen heroes, but it is interesting to note the characteristics that stand out. Jesus Christ would not qualify as a role model in these terms, neither for that matter would Mother Teresa nor Martin Luther King.

What is left out is as telling as what is included. A flick through the Gospels reveals that Jesus cried in public, had non-sexual friendships with women, refused violent action, forgave his enemies and gave up his life for his friends (See John 11:35; Luke 10:38-42, Mark 14:48-50; Luke 23:34; Mark 10:45). It's hard to imagine how this sort of behavior would fit into the Rambo, Bond or Jones image. Yet Jesus is the most complete picture of manhood we have. What has happened in the late twentieth century is that traditional macho "male" characteristics have been elevated to the virtual exclusion of so-called female qualities such as kindness, love and forgiveness.

Of course, every generation gets the heroes it wants. Bond and co. would not have achieved their enormous popularity unless the role models they offered were approved by modern cinema audiences. When we watch a film or video we may not be looking for role models, but by identifying with the hero we stand in their shoes and see the world through their eyes. How much they actually influence us on a subliminal level is a debate that will continue for many years to come. What is certain is that heroes play an important role for the millions of teenagers who are the bread-and-butter audience for the film and video industry. At a stage in their lives when they are most susceptible to examples, offering them combat machines (Rambo) or vigilantes (Batman) to copy, is not likely to ease the increasing violence in our society.

4
MODERN LOVE STORIES

The screenplay formula that arrives most often on a film producer's desk is probably the one that runs: boy meets girl, they fall in love, they separate and eventually, against all odds, are reunited in time for the credits. In many of the great screen love stories *(Casablanca, Gone with the Wind)* the ending is reversed to ensure that the audience is sent away clutching their tissues.

During the 60s the permissive age challenged the old romantic film formula. Some of the more forgettable films of the era seemed bent on inventing a new formula: "boy meets a dozen or more girls and sleeps with them all to the background of swinging pop music." The 60s did produce some classic love films like *The Graduate* but even these were determined to explore previously forbidden territory in sexual behavior.

In the 1980s the legacy of the permissive era can be seen in the way sex plays a much bigger part in romantic films. If boy meets girl and they fall in love it's accepted that we will cut to the bedroom before very long. Sex has become an essential part of the modern romantic film, where in the past it was hinted at but never actually shown.

Yet Hollywood finds itself in something of a no-man's land when it comes to the subject of love in the 80s and 90s. The old-fashioned love story, where the interest is in when and how the lovers will finally make it to the altar, is thought too coy and naive for our generation. On the other hand the 60s' assumption, that you should give your love away to each passing stranger as if it were no more than loose change, has been discredited. This may have something to do with the impact of the AIDS epidemic in our time, but it is also because most people have recognized by now that the 60s revolution was an empty victory. Satisfying love is not to be found in a series of sexual adventures.

Where does that leave male-female relationships in the present climate? Experiencing a great deal of anxiety and heart-searching is the answer. Relationship films in the 80s were notably less about fulfilling love than infidelity and break-up. A flood of films, some of which we'll look at in this chapter, dealt with marital unfaithfulness and its consequences. Thirty-something successes like *When Harry Met Sally* and many of Woody Allen's films obsessively rework the question of whether friendship between men and women is possible; does it always have to end up in bed?

Love and Be Happy

The essential question at the heart of all these films is, "Can men and women make each other happy?" If anyone were to analyze all the popular-song lyrics ever written they'd probably be forced to reach the conclusion that romantic love was the one and only key to happiness. The promises of advertising to deliver this happiness are based 90% on this assumption. If we drive the right car, spray on the right perfume or pour ourselves into the right brand of jeans, we will secure the man or woman of our dreams.

The quest for romantic love and sexual fulfillment remains one of the great driving forces of our age. "Sex with love is about the most beautiful thing there is," says heartthrob John Travolta, adding, "but sex without love isn't so bad either."[1]

If it is possible for men and women to be happy together, the next question is, how do they achieve it? How should the sexes relate to each other? In a Western society where both sexes are still trying to work out the implications of feminism, the answers are not straightforward and the ambiguities are reflected in the films we will look at. As John Ellis points out, "The masculine is assumed to be a set of positive definitions: action towards a goal, activity in the world, aggressiveness, heterosexual desire. This implies an opposite: the feminine. But the definition of the feminine remains a problem and is obsessively worked over in narrative fiction films."[2]

Falling in Love (1984)

Arguably the most accomplished actor and actress of the last decade—Robert De Niro and Meryl Streep—were paired together in this tale of a clandestine love affair. The film's stars guaranteed great expectations which the film never fully delivered, but it is still a telling example of Hollywood's attitudes to love and marriage.

The film begins and ends at Christmas; the bright lights and happy shoppers signal this will be a film about romantic love. We soon learn that both Streep and De Niro are married to other partners—of course, this is not a film about love *within* marriage—and the title refers to the romance of an affair.

Streep is a commercial artist and De Niro someone who wears hard-hats and spends a lot of time on building sites. (Ever noticed people never actually *work* in these films?) They meet accidentally in a bookstore and then coincidentally find they travel on the same train to work. The affair develops slowly, shyly and with many awkward moments. Streep and De Niro are never less than convincing in their roles and capture perfectly the self-conscious mannerisms of two people attracted to each other. But by showing the characters as weak and vulnerable in the opening scenes, the film is out to enlist our sympathy for the developing affair. Once this is achieved we are swept up in a whirl of romance with the lovers eating Chinese takeouts, playing in an amusement arcade and giggling together in a photo booth.

We cut to a silent meal shared at home between Streep and her doctor husband, Brian, "We had a woman die today," says Brian by way of conversation. The film seriously shortchanges the married partners on the receiving end of the affair. Streep's husband makes fleeting appearances wearing a perpetual killjoy sneer. De Niro's partner is allowed brief glimpses of personality, slapping him in the face when he breaks the news of his unfaithfulness. But we are not interested in their stories, this is a film about falling in love, and the uncomfortable reality of broken marriages does not merit a close look. The message is that love cannot endure in the humdrum atmosphere of married life; it needs the secret hot-house excitement of an affair to flourish in.

Redesigning Reality

There is little evidence of durable happiness in the relations between Streep and De Niro's characters however. Their be-havior has all the marks of teenage infatuation and most of the time they are living on the edge of their nerves—making secret phone calls, racing for trains, and driving through the pouring rain at night. *Falling in Love* is about the falling part of the title and has little to tell us about what sustains and develops love once infatuation has run its course. The ending of the film offers us no clues since we leave the couple re-united on a train, having conveniently ditched their marriage partners since they last saw each other.

It is perhaps asking too much of Hollywood to make a film that is an honest appraisal of love within a committed rela-tionship such as marriage (it is difficult to think of a modern example that isn't actually about divorce). What is dishonest about *Falling in Love,* and other films of the forbidden-affair variety, is that they present such a shallow romantic view of infidelity. Not only does the film gloss over the effects of the affair on the injured parties—the married partners and chil-dren—it also manipulates our sympathies toward the lovers in subtle ways.

One example is when the lovers try—and fail—to make love at a friend's house. Full marks for honest realism here, but the scene is immediately followed by a tender train ride home and Streep arriving to the news that her father has died. Our sympathy for the affair is further increased because Streep's husband can never seem to be reached on the phone when he's needed. Cue De Niro.

The mirror-image structure of the film also serves up life packaged in a neatly wrapped box. At the beginning Streep and De Niro both have been best friends who are getting out of relationships; at the end it so happens that these friends are both happily paired off again. Everything is designed to make us wish the two main characters into each other's arms.

Coincidences are nothing new in romantic films, but they are being employed here throughout to gloss over the dishonesty of the situation. "We were meant to be together," says Streep at one point. "It was the right thing. Everything else is wrong." Hollywood is kidding us by redesigning reality to fit around the needs of an affair and suggesting that this is the "happy-ever-after" solution.

Fatal Attraction (1987)

Fatal Attraction, the box-office smash of 1987, caused a sensation for including precisely what *Falling in Love* left out: a twist in the tale where betrayal in marriage gets what it deserves. That the idea should be thought so original in the late 80s says a lot about our society's casual acceptance of adultery.

The film bills itself as a terrifying love story—a mixture of the eternal triangle with a psycho-thriller twist. Many saw the film as anti-permissive coming as it did at the peak of AIDS hysteria in America.

The film opposes two worlds as almost black-and-white realities—the world of family relationships and the world of illicit sexual liaison. Dan Gallagher (Michael Douglas) has a choice between the two. Like many men, he initially believes he's entitled to have his cake and eat it, but the film acts as a savage reminder that male-female relationships don't come in threes.

The key to the film's attitudes comes in a scene where Alex Forest (Glen Close) spies on her lover's family. The parents and child are sitting around a cozy fireside. Both the little girl and her glamorous mother wear white and they are playing with a fluffy pet rabbit that Daddy has just brought home. Alex (wearing black) watches the scene and throws up. Whether this is a reaction to the sickly sweet depiction of family life in the film is not clear. It is more likely that Alex is meant to represent the jealous threat of the outsider to the family hearth. In this film, singles are lonely, dangerous people.

Too Hot to Handle

Alex's own home is presented in stark contrast. Gallagher follows her there when his wife is away for a weekend. Her apartment is in a shadowy district with fires burning in the street and raw meat hanging on hooks. Inside, an elevator takes them from a dark damp lobby to a flat with bare white walls. Their love-making is violent, passionate, and not confined to the conventionality of the bed. In what is by any standards a gratuitously explicit scene, the message is underlined that real sexual passion can only be found in the forbidden fruit of casual sex. Gallagher may desire his own wife but we note that his advances to *her* are always interrupted by their daughter or a ring at the door. Family life may be cozy but it lacks excitement.

However, the excitement soon turns too hot when Alex attempts suicide and continues to demand Dan's attention when his wife is back in town. "I think you're terrific but I'm married," he explains. "We're adults, you know the rules." This is where the film is at its most hard-hitting, showing the often opposing expectations of men and women in relationships. Gallagher's view of sex is of a simple, pleasurable experience without meaning or responsibility. In effect he denies that any relationship has taken place.

"You're sick," he tells Alex. "Why?" she asks. "Because I won't be treated like a slut, because I want some respect?" When Alex claims she is pregnant he assumes she'll have an abortion. The rules are different for men and women.

Casual Consequences

But infidelity has consequences, rightly shown here to be more than an unforeseen pregnancy. Gallagher begins by lying to his wife from the moment she arrives home. He then tells his secretary to lie to Alex that he is not in his office. The casual sin of one weekend spins itself out into a web of lies until Gallagher is caught and his happy marriage wrecked when his wife learns the truth. *Fatal Attraction* argues that we must take responsibility for our actions or eventually deceit will bring its own reward.

So far so good, but then the film shifts gear and Alex becomes a psycho-killer in the *Halloween* mold. Objects begin to acquire a Hitchcock sense of menace. Phones ring at moments of tension, hot water runs in the bathroom, the rabbit is found boiled alive and the kettle sings while Dan's wife screams upstairs. As a revenge thriller the film never misses a beat, but inevitably the issues raised are lost in the blood-and-terror climax. Any claims that Alex had as a woman abused are forfeited because she turns into a slasher madwoman wielding a bread knife. The family break-up caused by Gallagher's unfaithfulness is conveniently solved by his wife's need for male protection.

In the end, the film cheats on the profounder questions it raises and settles for a nail-biting thriller with the family as the good guys and single women as the villains. It ends with the police leaving the scene of the crime. Any decent detective would have had some awkward questions to ask. Is sex more than a physical art? Do men use women in relationships? Is adultery okay if you don't pick someone who is cruel to rabbits? *Fatal Attraction* is not telling.

Shirley Valentine (1989)

Shirley Valentine, Willy Russell's adaptation of the original stage play, was one of the surprise successes of 1989. Pauline Collins received an Oscar nomination for her portrayal of Shirley, and the film outran many bigger-budget films. If for no other reason, the film deserves inclusion here because it looks at relationships from a female viewpoint—a rarity in cinema.

Shirley is a suburban housewife in Liverpool. She has a husband, grown-up children, a comfortable house, and she is bored. John Ellis's view that the definition of the feminine remains a problem in films provides ample source material here. What do women want from life? Shirley only knows that whatever it is, she hasn't found it. She is her husband's wife and cook, her daughter's dependable mother, her friend's confidante, but she has lost touch with herself. Whatever happened to Shirley Valentine?

The question arises as a result of a chance encounter with
an old school friend. Shirley's image of the girl she always
envied at school—pretty, refined and the teacher's favorite—
is shattered when she discovers her friend is now a high-
class call-girl. The conformity and acceptance young Shirley
had always yearned for turns out to be an empty illusion.

More Than a Holiday Romance

She determines to find herself before it's too late. An escape
route offers itself in the form of a holiday on a Greek island
with her best friend. At first she appears to have simply
exchanged a wet climate for a sunnier one. Her friend deserts
her for a man, and Shirley sits on the beach talking to a rock.
She is constantly the victim of other people who expect her
to wait submissively in the background while they get on
with living. In a society where the masculine role is often
active and the feminine passive, Shirley voices the cry of
those who have lost their self-worth because they have no
part to play.

Much of the film's success hinges on Shirley's brilliant
comic monolog to her kitchen wall. Through this device Russell enables his heroine to directly address us, the audience.
This is a theatrical technique rarely used in cinema with any
success. One reason why it works so beautifully here is because Shirley's monologs strike a chord in all of us. Just as
children invent imaginary friends to talk to, Shirley longs for
someone that will actually *listen to her*. No matter how many
relationships we have, most of us have at some point felt this
sense of alienation and loneliness.

Finally the remedy for loneliness appears to come to her
table in the guise of a Greek taverna owner (Tom Conti). He

takes her out on his boat where she is willingly seduced by Greek wine and flattery. If the story ended here then the film would seem to agree with *Falling in Love* that if you don't find salvation in one relationship you should simply swap it for a better one. But Russell's screenplay and his heroine are too knowing for that.

Making Choices
Shirley refuses to return home to be condemned to four walls and cooking steak for her husband again. She turns back at the airport only to find her Greek lover is already employing the same line on a new English vacationer. Shirley stays on unperturbed; she has come away to find herself, not to play another role in someone else's life.

Russell's film is unusual in rejecting male-female relationships as the means of salvation and ultimate fulfillment. He points beyond this to a need for rebirth in each individual. Shirley Valentine may not experience a spiritual awakening but she certainly comes to the awareness that we have been created as free beings who must strive to achieve our own potential. It is not enough to pass life by, playing a minor role within other people's dreams.

The film ends with a hint that this rebirth of the individual could take place within marriage if the two sides are willing to recognize their partner's need to retain a separate identity. At the same time *Shirley Valentine* is one of the few films to voice the possibility that the single state can be a happy one. We don't all need relationships with the opposite sex to be fulfilled.

What conclusions can be drawn from these three films about the nature of love relationships between men and women? The first must be that they are an uncertain thing to base happiness upon. Each of the films contains an adulterous relationship and in only one does the original marriage look certain to survive. Hollywood of course is the place "where brides keep the bouquet and throw away the groom,"[3] so we shouldn't be surprised if it presents a jaundiced view of marriage.

Nevertheless each film in its own way represents a search for personal fulfillment that is never satisfied by sexual love within or without marriage. Women are often represented as victims of male dominance, and men grow restless once the thrill of the chase is past. Perhaps what all love-story films are really saying is that human relationships must be a shadow of something they've not yet found. When Shirley Valentine talks to her wall she is dreaming of something more than the ideal lover. What she really desires is someone or something to offer reassurance of her own worth and identity. Russell's film suggests the answer lies within ourselves. Christians point to God as the missing piece in the jigsaw. In St. Augustine's words, "Thou hast made us for thyself and the heart of man is restless till it finds its rest in thee."

5
NIGHTMARES ARE FUN

"As far as God goes, I'm a non-believer. . . . But when it comes to the Devil—well that's something else . . . the Devil keeps advertising. . . . The Devil does lots of commercials."

Thus writes William Peter Blatty in *The Exorcist,* which became one of the biggest and most controversial of modern horror movies. The statement raises an interesting question—how come films that deal with God and his intervention in the earthly realm are so rare, whereas films that deal with the Devil, demons, zombies, spirits and spooks are too numerous to mention?

Human beings are apparently fascinated by evil and are prepared to spend large amounts of money in search of the ultimate hair-raising experience. Horror flicks represent fear within safe limits. If Freddy Krueger, Dracula or any of their bloodthirsty army were really to turn up in our bedrooms our fascination would quickly evaporate, but we know they are phantoms of light who can't reach out from the screen and grab us.

The insatiable demand for horror films, then, may be a way of dealing with our own irrational fears through the lives of actors on a screen. Most of us fear the creak on the stair at night, and we would rather watch someone else open the door and go out to investigate. Encountering the axe-man or monster in film fantasy, we somehow ward him off from real life.

Horrific Realities

This may in part explain the popularity of bogeyman films like *Halloween* and *Nightmare on Elm Street* where the thrill is to experience the fear of the victim. But what about the films that delve deeper into the dark side of the supernatural? Money makers from *The Exorcist* to *Ghostbusters* and *The Witches of Eastwick* have turned to the occult world for their scary monsters. From a commercial viewpoint this is no doubt a logical step—the Devil is after all the ultimate bogeyman. But at a deeper level the popularity of these films says something about human nature. While audiences often find any portrayal of God and goodness hard to take in films, they eagerly welcome each new gruesome ghoul. The Bible finds a reason for this within our own natures; "men loved darkness instead of light because their deeds were evil" (John 3:19).

It doesn't necessarily follow that any film that falls within the broad definition of horror is unsavory and best avoided (although anyone is entitled to act on this view). Some films scare because they bring out frightening truths. When Dr.

Frankenstein or Seth Brundle *(The Fly)* have the pride to think they can imitate God, then the results are a chilling warning of what happens when human beings set themselves in the place of their Creator.

The litmus test in examining the horror genre is to ask what is the nature of reality as reflected in the film's world? How are good and evil represented? Does the film relish death and pain inflicted on humanity or present it as a warning? These are the sort of questions we'll look at in reviewing some of the modern horror favorites of recent years.

Halloween 1-4 (1978-1989)

When the first *Halloween* movie was released in 1978 no one could foresee that John Carpenter's low-budget quickie would go on to earn $18.5 million in America alone and release a tidal wave of successors all eager to cash in on the latest trend.

Halloween is basically a psycho-killer story—you can't kill the bogeyman—as the posters gleefully warned. Variations on the maniac-menaces-girl-in-claustrophobic-situations are, as Kim Newman puts it, "about as original as an Italian Western re-make of a samurai epic."[1] Yet like *A Fistful of Dollars* the film-going public lapped this one up. Carpenter's success was perhaps partly due to encapsulating one simple idea in the title. "Halloween cannot promise anything sedate and Halloween is to menace what sugar is to gratification."[2]

The original *Halloween* plot (rehashed in most of the sequels) is as simple as making a pumpkin lantern. Michael Myers, a dangerous psycho, breaks out of the asylum on Halloween night and heads for his hometown. Dr. Loomis (Donald Pleasence), his slightly crazed psychiatrist, sets off in pursuit. When Michael gets to Haddonfield he scares a lot of people, kills three high-school kids and terrorizes Jamie Lee Curtis as his next intended victim.

The only original variation on countless other psychothrillers is that Michael eventually turns into "the Shape," an unkillable version of the bogeyman. *Halloween* therefore acquires a supernatural dimension where evil is somehow unbeatable. Jamie Lee Curtis is allowed the triumph of escaping with her life but we know Myers will be back in the next sequel to menace another heroine. The nightmare characters of Myers, Freddy and co. have it all their own way—there is no suggestion that opposing spiritual forces of good are part of the picture. Evil is on the loose and can only be temporarily held at bay. The Christian view that the crucifixion inflicted a once-and-for-all defeat on the forces of darkness (Hebrews 10:10-14) would imply a possible end to the nightmare (and its sequels). But the heroines of *Halloween* and *Elm Street* have only their own resources to call on. An uneven contest in which everybody else comes to a bloody end.

A Catalog of Horrors

Halloween 1 was not the worst of the horror-slasher films by any means. Carpenter lends the film pace, an eerie atmosphere and effects that jolt the audience, such as characters leaping out of the corner of a frame. The most disturbing effect of the film was that it unleashed a whole glut of imitations, led by *Friday the 13th*, that were less squeamish about the way they exploited their audience in the pursuit of making a fast buck.

As Newman points out, the conventions of this subgenre of horror are as rigid as in any Harlequin romance[3] and are worth noting as they apply to many of the big, horror money-makers that are still spawning endless sequels.

☐ There is often a date referred to in the title *(Mother's Day, Graduation Day, Friday the 13th,* etc.).

☐ The cast is dominated by American adolescents left over from earlier teen sex films such as *Porky's, Meatballs,* etc. They are marked as victims by indulgence in sex, drink and drugs.

☐ In order to build up suspense and get to the horror sequences, all the characters must act like idiots. *Friday the 13th* and *Nightmare on Elm Street* are full of teenagers wandering around in the dark in search of a good place to be attacked.

☐ The camera gives us the killer's-eye view of his victims.

☐ The plot is basically a string of explicit, blood-drenched murders.

The mindless reproduction of these conventions in so many films is worrying in a number of ways. Firstly, the films are obviously aimed at the large and impressionable young teen-age audience. What is served up is simply a cinematic roller-coaster ride, high on sex, violence and blood splattering. Secondly, there is a relish about the violent content that reduces it to the level where audiences laugh out loud. In *Halloween 3* bodies are consumed by snakes and worms, fried alive and set on fire, culminating in a scene where a girl is decapitated with a blunt instrument. The view of human life is that it's as expendable as fake blood. The films desensitize us to thinking and feeling about violence in a real way.

You As the Killer
Even worse is the fact that we are asked to enjoy playing the

role of gruesome killer ourselves. By tracking the victims using a camera giving us the killer's viewpoint, we enjoy the thrill of the chase and the scent of the kill as if it were our own.

The honest label for this sort of film is soft porn for the teenage market. Horror films like *Dracula* have always contained erotic impulses, but recently they have moved to a wholehearted imitation of the structure of the porno film. Often the murders are sex-killings. Michael Myers in *Halloween* exclusively chooses promiscuous teenagers as his victims. Freddy Krueger, too, turns up immediately following bedroom scenes. There is a sexual voyeurism at work here masquerading as anti-permissiveness. Myers kills everyone but Laurie, the one virgin in the film. On the surface it appears that psycho films are a warped kind of warning against promiscuity, but often the pure heroine is the one who becomes the killer's main target. Killing becomes a metaphor for sexual initiation, and the whole appeal of the movie is to see whether the heroine will give in to sexual temptation or get murdered.

The undercurrent in films like *Dracula* and *Halloween* is not anti-permissive but rather a gross distortion of sexuality. Sex becomes closely linked with violent assault of female victims. The fact that the killer becomes a supernatural indestructible monster suggests that moral or physical resistance is in the end useless. Although virginal heroines often survive, a view of sex that associates it with blades, razor claws and dripping blood is one that distorts its place. In a Christian view of creation, sex is not only a valued gift of the Creator but a gift freely given by both married partners (Ephesians 5:28-31).

Nightmare on Elm Street (1984-1990)

Just when it seemed the psycho film had played itself out, along came Freddy Krueger. Freddy's trademarks are a battered hat, a striped sweater, wickedly long nails and a fried face. As a monster there is something comically grotesque about him which the character plays on with a lewd, leering personality. Freddy's history is that of a child-murdering caretaker, burned alive in a boiler room by vengeful parents. He reminds us of nothing so much as the dirty old man of the neighborhood, the bogeyman that all parents tell their children to watch out for.

The modest twist supplied by the *Elm Street* venture is that Freddy inhabits the world of our nightmares and is summoned when we sleep. This provides a good excuse for surreal special effects where claws shoot out of the bath water and tongues from the phone receiver. Freddy's first victim, Tina, pays for making love to her boyfriend by her stomach bursting open and being dragged around the ceiling in a bath of blood. Another victim is sucked down into a hole in his bed whereupon a geyser of blood erupts onto the ceiling. This sort of effect is over the top, if not downright silly, but it illustrates the lengths films are now having to go to get a reaction from an audience. Where once it was thought daring to see a stake plunged into Dracula's heart, now audiences are not satisfied unless the gore is graphic and served up in bucketfuls. Again the underlying message is that death and pain are meaningless fun.

"Dreams," as a scientist in the film explains rather technically, "are mysteries, incredible body hocus-pocus." The only thing we know for certain is that they come from somewhere within us. It follows that Freddy is an extension of our imagination. Nancy, the film's heroine, thinks she can kill Freddy at the end by turning her back on him—"I want my mother and my friends again. I take back every bit of energy I ever gave you." In this respect the *Elm Street* films present Freddy as a type of the Devil whom we can resist or give a foothold in our lives according to the choices we make. However, the only power Nancy needs is the power of positive thinking; again the forces of light get no more mention than a token crucifix above Nancy's bed.

The film closes with the inevitable "Was it a dream or wasn't it?" ending, leaving us with the impression that it has all been an excuse for the special effects and make-up departments to look forward to healthy business for some time.

Poltergeist (1982)

Where *Halloween* and *Elm Street* merely dabble with supernatural variations on a psycho theme, *Poltergeist* launched itself wholeheartedly into exploring "the other side." The original film, although directed by Tobe Hooper, bears all the marks of cowriter Steven Spielberg's influence. In many ways it is the dark-dream equivalent of *E.T.* using the same sweet, suburban family (complete with three cute kids and a dog), this time invaded by unfriendly ghosts.

The scenario owes much to the haunted-house tradition, with the difference that the house is part of a sprawling suburban estate in mid-America. The ghosts are also different—poltergeists—noisy ghosts who are spirits of the dead trapped in limbo above the earth before they can cross over into the light. *Poltergeist,* despite its heavy reliance on special effects, has pretensions to being a serious psychic-phenomena film that confronts questions of what exists after death.

The film introduces itself with the "Stars and Stripes" anthem playing while the "ghosts" of TV images are shown in eerie close-up. Spielberg has always had a fascination for the modern magic of electricity, and here it is the TV set which is the agent of chaos in the Freeling family home. After the credits Carol Ann, the youngest of the children, is seen talking to the screen.

TV Channels

Television is the ever-present idol of the Freeling family. It is always on in the background introducing flickering images of war to Carol Ann when she stops to watch. The Freelings, too, are at war with their neighbor over the interference of his remote control with their television. Adults watching football shout at the screen in the same way Carol Ann talks to the invisible TV people. Ultimately it is the television that introduces the ghosts into the house and imprisons the little girl inside where her voice can be heard calling to her parents.

It is ironic that Spielberg, the crown prince of modern mass-communication, has conceived a ghost-story parable warning against the mass media becoming modern idols that disrupt the relationships of family life. On a simple level the message is that TV can have a hypnotic unseen effect on children. A deeper reading of the film would be to connect the dangerous fascination with the occult today with the increasing intrusion of the mass media into everyday life. "The absence of a TV signal means it's open to receive all sorts of things," explains one of the psychic experts. In the same way hours of television messages can assume a powerful influence in our lives if there is nothing stronger there to take their place. By the end of the film, Steve Freeling dumps the motel TV set outside in the rain. The fact that the action seems so extreme to modern audiences underlines just how secure an idol TV has become in our generation.

Poltergeist is not just about the threat of modern machinery to human life, it also plunges the Freelings into the uncertain world of spirits. A suitably weird psychic expert is drafted in to explain reality beyond the grave—"There's no death, only a transition to a sphere of different consciousness." If this seems unhelpfully vague she adds, "Some believe that when you die there's a wonderful light. . . . But some people get lost on their way to the light, and they need someone to guide them to it." We are told that spirits caught in limbo have been attracted to Carol Ann's life-force and need her help to find a window into the light.

Pick Your Own Religion

Like most filmmakers Spielberg and Hooper like to trade on elements of religion but mix and match them to come up with a pseudo-spiritual creed that suits the film's story line. There are elements here of God/Christ as the light destination and the Devil as the beast trying to prevent a soul's salvation. The idea of limbo is also borrowed from Catholic belief in a region for unbaptized babies and the righteous who died before Christ. All this is crammed into a world beyond the bedroom door, and Spielberg comes up with the solution of throwing in a few tennis balls and a rope down which Carol Ann escapes with her mother covered in slime. As an exhibition of special effects, the sequence is masterful, but as a clue to what lies on the other side of death it's as much use as a rubber ring with a puncture.

Poltergeist finishes with a tacked-on ending (probably Hooper's) where all hell literally breaks loose. Skeletons surface in the swimming pool, coffins erupt in the house, a giant oesophagus attempts to swallow the family and finally the house implodes into nothing. Amidst the special effects, Steve points the finger at the boss of the housing corporation who built the estate on the site of a cemetery—"You moved the headstones but left the bodies!" he shouts. The real villain of this horror is not a mad doctor or vengeful monster but the greed of big corporations.

Ghostbusters (1984)

To conclude this sample of modern horror it's interesting to compare the supernatural threat of wandering spirits in *Poltergeist* with the apocalyptic spooks of the original *Ghostbusters*.

Ghostbusters does not properly belong within the horror category but the climax of the film offers a sort of *"National Lampoon* meets the *Devil Rides Out"* which belongs squarely within the tradition of devil movies. Now that Hollywood's obsession with demon possession has exhausted itself, *Ghostbusters* represents a possible trend toward apocalyptic movies.

Ghostbusters casts Bill Murray, Dan Aykroyd and Harold Ramis as a trio of parapsychologists ridding Manhattan of a wave of ghoulish pests. For much of the film the ghosts are no worse than green jelly-blobs with a weakness for hot dogs. Toward the end, however, the Book of Revelation is called in to provide more worthy opponents for our heroes. As Newman explains, "A 1930s skyscraper in the middle of New York has been constructed by an evil architect to act as a gateway to another dimension. Now a horde of Sumerian demons are flooding through Sigourney Weaver's fridge to wreak havoc of Old Testament proportions on the Big Apple."[4]

The film is a wacky comedy vehicle for Murray and company which nobody could take too seriously, but it reflects the other extreme from *Poltergeist*'s psychic pretensions, where the occult is now seen as one big joke. "I think it's a sign from God—but don't quote me on that," says a cardinal while nuns with rosary beads and Jewish rabbis cheer the arrival of the Ghostbusters. Weaver becomes a high priestess and Gozer, the chief demon, appears in female form with a dog's voice. A giant marshmallow-man stalks New York like King Kong, only to be toasted by the ectoplasmic flamethrowers. It is all harmless nonsensical stuff but highlights the way all supernaturalism, from jelly-blob ghosts to biblical prophecy, is grist to the Hollywood mill.

Good Triumphs

The only certainty in all horror films is that the ultimate solution—whether to escaping the psycho or saving the world—lies in human courage and resourcefulness rather than a divine savior. The spiritual powers of light never feature as more than minor roles in the supernatural framework of film. "I love Jesus' style," says the black (and therefore religious) recruit to Ghostbusters. But Jesus apparently has no role to play in the apocalyptic fight against evil demons.

The litmus test, we said earlier, is to ask what is the nature of reality according to the world of the films? Reality, if we are to believe them, has a supernatural dimension that is populated by spirits, demons and murderous half-human ghouls. On the existence of dark forces (whatever their nature) Christians can agree (Ephesians 6:12). Where the horror films fall woefully short is in showing the other side of the spiritual realm. Without any reference to a loving God and the saving power of his Son the picture makes no sense. If the world of the horror film were reality then evil would be rampant everywhere and human beings powerless to resist. This is potentially the most sinister effect of watching horror films—we may eventually begin to believe that evil is in total control.

Christians would do well to remember the warning of *The Exorcist:* "The Devil does lots of commercials."

6 WAR GAMES

| **"When Hollywood goes to war it usually drops bombs."**

So said one critic of the film industry's poor record on war films. In no other type of film can the difference between reality and the Hollywood version of history be seen so clearly.

Yet war has always been a popular subject for the cinema to turn its cameras on. Whether it's the historical pageantry of knights in armor, the cannons firing in the Crimea, the cowboys chased by whooping Indians or heroics against the "Hun" in the Second World War, war has always proved a good draw at the box office.

When you consider the horrific reality of war brought into our homes in modern times by documentary footage of Vietnam and other wars, the question has to be asked, "Why do we enjoy watching war films?" Over the last decade the number of films to come out of the American experience in Vietnam has turned from a trickle into a tidal wave.

Some would say our society is simply obsessed with violence. Violence in the cinema is a modern epidemic, they argue, citing the Rambo school of philosophy that there is nothing like a little wholesale slaughter for building up an appetite before lunch. The best of the Vietnam films, however (including the two considered in this chapter), fall into a different category. They are trying to comprehend the experience of war, not to glorify it.

Why Watch War?

Early in *The Deer Hunter* a mother pleads with her parish priest. "I do not understand, Father. I understand nothing any more. Can anyone explain?" This was the first film to honestly reflect the mood of a nation who had sent its sons to fight a war that could never be won.

There may be several answers to the question, "Why do we go to see war films?" Some of the answers may be too uncomfortable to admit. Yet, in the case of the films considered here, at least one answer must be that we go to try to understand.

Today we have more information than ever before. But all the armies of news commentators cannot explain to us the meaning of the fragmented events of war that flash across our TV screens. Film has the ability to make connections for us. It can take reality and present it as a whole that we can understand and identify with. War films raise important questions that come into sharp focus where human life is at stake. What is a person worth? Do widely accepted moral values still apply under conditions of war? If so, how do we know right and wrong? The veneer of civilized society is stripped away to reveal what humankind is like under the skin. Then are we left with an animal, a killing machine or a human being with a moral instinct that is a reflection of our Creator?

The Deer Hunter (1978)

For years after *The Deer Hunter* was released the actor Christopher Walken would be stopped in the street by people putting an imaginary gun to their heads in imitation of the Russian roulette sequence in the film. In fact, this part of the film had no roots in reality. There is no evidence that games of Russian roulette were forced upon American prisoners during the Vietnam war. Nevertheless the image is one people remembered. It represented so much about a war that seemed ultimately to be a futile gamble with the lives of men.

Hope and Hell

The Deer Hunter unfolds like a symphony in three parts. The first movement explores life in small-town America, the second takes us into the nightmare of Vietnam, and the third brings us full circle to witness the effect of war on the community of Clairton.

The film begins with a vision of hell; men in asbestos armor moving in a furnace of flames. This is the steel mill, the heart of Clairton's community. The main characters, three young steelworkers, are introduced to us via the rituals of hunting and a wedding.

The wedding, in a close-knit Eastern Orthodox community, is presented with vitality and affection. But the groom, Steven, has volunteered for Vietnam alongside his friends

Michael and Nick. The shadow of the war hangs over the celebrations. A banner at the reception reads "Serving God and country proudly" but the heroes can no more explain why they are going to war than Steven knows why he is marrying a woman who is carrying another man's child. The wedding is carried along by ritual rejoicing and naive optimism. The film implies that America entered the Vietnam war in the same spirit.

Two incidents at the wedding warn of the disillusionment in store. The bride and groom are invited to drink a ritual glass of wine—"If you don't spill a drop it's good luck for the rest of your life." The camera captures three red spots that escape onto the bride's dress. There is also an uninvited guest at the wedding—a green-bereted soldier who sits at the bar, a figure of doom to compare with the Ancient Mariner. When accosted, the only tale he has to tell is an obscene comment— the only statement of skepticism in the film's first section.

Facing the Vietcong

The second section also opens with fire, this time the hellfire of napalm bombs exploding around Michael who appears like an avenging angel through the flames. He does not even recognize Steve and Nick when they arrive and greet him. War has reduced Michael to a killing machine programmed only for survival. It will take the rest of the film for him to find his way back to full humanity.

Soon after, the three are captured by the Vietcong. The film omits the usual combat sequences in favor of the harrowing scene where the prisoners are forced to play Russian roulette by their captors. Here the tenor of war is distilled into one image—a gun pointed at the head with one bullet in the chamber. (It was inspired by the war's most famous news photo showing a suspected Vietcong being executed in a busy Saigon street.) Back home the friends had gambled on life as a joke. They bet on TV football and the chances of passing a truck on the inside without causing an accident. For their Vietcong captors the roulette is just the same kind of joke. They laugh when a prisoner blows his brains out.

Both sides are guilty of treating human life as expendable—without value or significance. The attitude spreads like a disease in the film to the point where Nick finally loses his life on the roulette gamble. Murder and suicide are carried out as casually as scratching an itch. War has reduced morality to a simple question of survival so that a human being is no better than an animal.

No Escape
The friends escape their captors but the film goes on to show there is no escape from the toll that war exacts on the individual. Michael's homecoming is a grim parody of the hero's send-off at the start of the film. He sneaks into town in the back of a taxi, avoiding his welcome party to hide in a gloomy motel. War has made him into a misfit, isolated from his community by the memories he carries. Steven's scars are physical as well as mental, and he prefers the safety of a veteran's hospital to facing the world outside. Nick never returns at all, and the senseless manner of his death hits the community hardest.

In all the tragedy, *The Deer Hunter*'s great strength is in its tenderness for its characters. At the beginning they are optimistic, naive and confident that they can win their bet on life. By the end nobody in the community is untouched

by the war. The final scene contrasts the awkward ritual of
the funeral meal with the earlier wedding feast. The survi-
vors gather together and sing "God Bless America." After
what has gone before, the words seem heavy with irony but
in fact the film achieves a moving testimony to the human
capacity for hope against all odds. Friendship, loyalty and
love of country still survive and suffering has purged the
characters of naiveté and bravado.

Above all *The Deer Hunter* affirms the value of life. It is
not to be casually decided on the spin of a bullet chamber or
the speed of a car. The film climaxes with a scene played out
to choral music and shot through with religious significance.
Michael, face to face with a deer he has been hunting in the
mountains, deliberately fires into the air. "Okay?" he roars at
the heavens. Killing is no longer a game. Life is sacred because it is charged with the grandeur of God.

Platoon (1987)

Oliver Stone's *Platoon* was finally acclaimed almost a decade
after *The Deer Hunter.* Stone, who fought in Vietnam him-
self, had wanted to make the film for some years but had to
wait until the climate was judged right to receive it. Where
The Deer Hunter has only a middle section set in Vietnam,
Stone's film sets itself in the war zone from beginning to end.
Platoon won four Oscars, including Best Picture and Best
Director.

The film is less ambitious than *The Deer Hunter.* It con-
cerns itself purely and simply with the realities of modern
warfare and its effect on the soldiers doing the fighting.
Stone chooses as his vehicle a raw recruit, Chris Taylor coming to Vietnam fresh from college to "do my bit for my coun-

try like Grandpa in World War Two."

The film traces Taylor's baptism into the army and his subsequent acceptance into the ranks of the Vietnam Vets. The question the film poses is, "What makes a good soldier?" It goes beyond professional ability to ask if there can be any meaningful morality for those fighting a war.

The platoon's lieutenant is a fresh-faced college product, uncomfortable with his authority over older men and unable to speak the brutal language of the barracks room. The battle for leadership of the platoon therefore falls to the two sergeants—Barnes and Elias. These two represent opposing models for Taylor as a soldier. Barnes is a hardened veteran who has long ago left morality behind as excess baggage in the battle for survival. Elias, on the other hand, acknowledges other laws besides the law of the jungle.

Fighting Ourselves

Taylor's verdict at the end of the film is, "We did not fight the enemy, we fought ourselves, the enemy within ourself." His statement echoes the Christian view of humanity. We are neither wholly good nor wholly bad but a battle rages within us between our God-given desires and our fallen nature. The law at work is the same one the apostle Paul discovered, "When I want to do good, evil is right there with me" (Romans 7:21).

In the crucible of war the restraints of society are stripped away and the man beneath the uniform is seen plainly. *Platoon* paints a dark picture of the result. At one point a teenage soldier uses his rifle butt to smash the head of a young Vietnamese with the crazed bravado of a schoolboy showing his friends he has the "guts" to do it.

Barnes is the full realization of the soldier as professional killer; ultimately he is willing to kill even his own side (Elias) if it serves his purpose. Taylor's dilemma is whether to take revenge for his friend's death. In the film's climax he walks in silence, blackened and bloodied among the bodies to find Barnes, wounded but still alive. "Do it," says Barnes, and Taylor's gun obliges.

The film's attitude to this final act of murder is ambiguous. Are we meant to approve the revenge of Elias or conclude that Taylor the raw recruit has graduated into the Barnes school of amorality? There is a suspicion that Stone wants to have it both ways—to condemn the bloodthirstiness of the platoon against innocent civilians but allow the revenge murder of a bad man. This way chaos lies. If all human life has dignity and value, then exceptions cannot be made for the treatment of bad men. Jesus' teaching—that even a criminal is capable of redemption (Luke 23:39-44)—is founded in God's unconditional mercy, not in whether our lives deserve to be shown mercy.

Platoon is almost a parable of good and evil in its characters. Yet even the cruelty of Barnes is overshadowed by the universal evil which is war itself. In *Platoon*'s dark world, the nearest thing to hope ever expressed is that if there is a heaven Elias will be sitting up there drunk and smoking pot. It's not a lot to look forward to.

The Killing Fields (1984)

A person charting the history of the late twentieth century through film could be forgiven for thinking that Vietnam was the only war that took place. *The Killing Fields* was a rare success about another war—this time in Cambodia.

The film is based on the real life relationship between Dith Pran, a Cambodian, and Sidney Shanberg, a journalist for the *New York Times*. It is unusual not only in choosing a central character who isn't a Westerner but also for showing war through the eyes of the media. Throughout we are conscious of cameras filming cameras at work. A photographer snaps maimed and bleeding bodies when a bomb goes off. We are both shocked and at the same time reminded of our own indifference to war as it's relayed to us secondhand by TV and press coverage.

The Killing Fields divides into two distinct halves. The first explores the relationship between Shanberg and Pran, his assistant, in their attempts to cover the war in Cambodia. The second half sees Pran left to the mercies of the Khmer Rouge in Cambodia while Shanberg collects accolades for his war stories in America.

Betrayal

The film's theme is betrayal, both on a personal and national level. Shanberg's assurances to Dith Pran and ultimate failure to safeguard his future are cleverly paralleled with America's abandonment of Cambodia to the infamous Pol Pot regime.

When Shanberg learns of the imminent American withdrawal he tells Pran that his family should leave. Pran, however, elects to stay on with the other journalists. Back in America, Shanberg will confess privately, "I never really gave him any choice. He stayed because I wanted him to stay." In war a moral evasion can lead to the death of the innocent. Shanberg doesn't lie to Pran, but neither does he impress on him the danger of staying. The journalist's half-truth is a telling example of how we dress sin up in other clothes to hide it from our conscience. Shanberg spends the rest of the film trying to appease his guilt with a publicity campaign to find his Cambodian friend.

The truth on a national scale is no more comfortable. Like Pran, his countrymen are victims of their innocent trust in the West. "In America everybody have a good time. Mercedes number one," a soldier informs Shanberg. When a U.S. bomber accidentally sheds its load on a civilian village, a girl innocently asks, "Did someone arrest the pilot?" Meanwhile Nixon appears on television assuring his audience, "There are no American troops in Cambodia. Cambodia is the Nixon doctrine in its purest form."

The Killing Fields is made with deliberate realism, often reminding us of documentary footage of war. Its style makes no attempt to simplify the confusing images of war. By adopting this approach it constantly warns us of the dangers of accepting media-packaged truth. When the bomber destroys a civilian village we see the press corps brought in and presented with a U.S.-sanitized version of the story via a commentary over the public address system. Later we see the same messages over loudspeakers used by the Khmer Rouge to preach its slogans of mindless obedience to Onga.

Charades

Throughout, the film highlights the charades played by the media in attempting to give us "the news." The BBC broadcasts updates from their "on the spot reporter" Hugh Elder who offers such euphemisms as "The situation is increasingly precarious." Those journalists actually left in Pnomh Penh joke about how the mysterious Elder is managing to smuggle his stories out.

The Killing Fields ends with a scene where Pran and Shanberg are reunited. "Imagine" by John Lennon, a modern anthem of peace, plays from a radio as Shanberg asks Pran, "Do you forgive me?" It is a rare instance in modern film of this line being spoken. Love, hate, anger and jealousy are favorite themes of cinema, but forgiveness is often the missing element. In a film which has turned on national and personal betrayal in war, Pran's simple embrace of Shanberg without a hint of bitterness, provides a moving and optimistic conclusion.

Like *Platoon* and *The Deer Hunter, The Killing Fields* can only relate war to us through the agency of individuals caught up in it. This is both the limitation and the strength of the film medium. In reducing war to a human scale it thus enables us to understand that wars are initiated and fought by individuals. It is the conflict between good and evil in each of us which is the war that is the father of all wars. In each of the films we see humans reduced to the level of animals or instruments of war. But in each we also catch a glimpse of the highest instincts of humanity—the potential for hope, self-sacrifice and loyalty to others that are a reflection of the fact that we are made in the image of a just God (Genesis 1:27).

7
HISTORY IN
THE MAKING

When George Lucas started making *Star Wars* he had the problem of constructing miniature model spacecrafts which convinced audiences that they were the real thing. Directors trying to turn history into cinema face a more mind-numbing problem of scale. How do you shrink the complex network of events and personalities that make up history into a two-hour motion picture?

It is not surprising that fiction and fantasy win hands down at the box office over true stories. Richard Attenborough, director of *Ghandi* and *Cry Freedom,* explains, "Film financiers, in the main, are nervous of any subject of real substance. They are convinced that audiences around the world wish only to be 'entertained' and that anything which

challenges their views or engages their intelligence as well
as their hearts is a potentially dangerous box office propo-
sition."[1]

Even if the backing is there, directors of films based on
fact are caught on the horns of a dilemma. If they pay too
little attention to history the films will be criticized as inac-
curate; if they include too much complicated detail the films
may flop as boring. History is full of charismatic leading
players, but it also includes a frustrating number of walk-on
parts that would call for a cast of thousands.

The natural solution for any filmmaker is to select from
history what can be used and to invent whatever else is
necessary. Of course, every filmmaker has to decide what the
limits of invention are. One example of this is the scene in
Chariots of Fire where Eric Liddell meets the Prince of
Wales and comes under royal pressure to run on the Sabbath. The scene is crucial to building the dramatic tension of
Liddell's situation, but in reality the meeting never took
place.

What is at stake here is a question of truth. No method of
communication, whether textbook or Hollywood movie, can
be expected to unroll history before us with the accuracy of
a map. On the other hand, the director who is dealing with
real people and events must accept some duty to be faithful
to the truth. For Christians watching such films it is as well
to remind ourselves that we are always watching *someone's
view of history* and to check on the evidence presented.

Real Events
The three films in this chapter—*Cry Freedom, Mississippi
Burning* and *The Last Emperor* all choose to view historical

events through the eyes of one or two central characters. This is a time-honored method (Shakespeare and Tolstoy did the same) which has its own advantages and disadvantages. On the one hand, the broad sweep of history will only be conveyed in as far as it affects the main characters. (Without background knowledge *The Last Emperor* is sometimes difficult to follow in this respect.) On the other hand, the events of history are given their full emotional impact since we'll identify with the characters we have gotten to know.

Each of the three films is based on real events in the twentieth century. Each has its own view of history—explicitly or implicitly stated in the way events are presented. Is history random and meaningless? An attempt to build an earthly paradise or a record of God's dealings with humanity? If every picture tells a story, what kind of history books do these pictures make?

Cry Freedom (1987)

Cry Freedom was born out of two books written by the exiled South African newspaper editor Donald Woods. At the core of the film is the leader of the Black Consciousness Movement, Steve Biko, who died in police custody in 1977. *Cry Freedom* is not a biography of Biko, however; the focus is as much on Woods and his conversion from well-meaning liberal to outspoken activist.

Attenborough's film never lets us forget its roots in reality; typewritten headlines giving the dates of the original events are repeatedly punched across the screen. But this is history interpreted differently by two opposing sides. "Biko's death leaves me cold. He died after a hunger strike," proclaims Justice Minister Kruger to a cheering audience after Biko has sustained massive brain damage from beatings in his cell. As the film ends the final roll call of black prisoners who died in custody by "falling down stairs" or "slipping in the shower" rams the messsage home—history can always be rewritten by those who control the power of communication.

The lesson of history as taught by Captain De Wet (Timothy West) and the South African authorities is that might is right, as long as it has a white face. The most harrowing scene—when the police open fire on the schoolchildren's strike in Lesotho—is saved until the end. A police car is shown chasing a child trying to run away, while the marksman in the car takes careful aim. The image stays in the mind long after the film. History may be ruled in the short term by those with their finger on the trigger, but in the end barbarity will reap its own reward.

Attenborough remains an optimist about the future of humanity. He does not believe that evil, however well armed, can ultimately triumph. Although Biko's death is represented as an appalling tragedy, it comes halfway through the film. It is Wood's crusade to tell his friend's story that makes Biko's name a rallying point for black people, not only in South Africa but throughout the continent.

The turning point for Woods himself, comes when he is proclaimed a banned person, like Biko, surrounded by invisible barbed wire, with the police always watching just across the street. He decides to write a book—Biko's biography—and smuggle it out of South Africa. The 400-mile journey is a race against time. Woods though, has already made a more difficult journey inside himself—from his affluent, white, middle-class background to the point of sacrificing it all in the fight to see justice extended to the black majority.

Taking Sides

Like all real sacrifices the cost is high and is also borne by others. His children are sent T-shirts impregnated with acid; his wife, Wendy, receives obscene phone calls, and the whole family is uprooted from its native land in order to get the book published. *Cry Freedom* underlines the old truth that in order for evil to triumph it is only necessary that good men and women do nothing. Further, it shows that good people have to suffer before they can truly help those suffering. Only when Woods is deprived of his own freedom can he begin to be of real use in the struggle for equality in South Africa.

As a retelling of history the film cannot hide its partisan roots. The portrayal of Biko—from his first appearance, silhouetted against bright sunlight—is rather idealized. Denzel Washington's Biko only comes to life in his public speeches, and the ambiguous relationship with the beautiful Dr. Ramphele is glossed over. Attenborough's film is at its best when conveying its sense of outrage at the way police and government gang up against justice in South Africa. Like most films based on fact, *Cry Freedom* has something to say, and homes in on the points in history which most forcefully support its argument.

South Africa is a country where blacks and whites have both claimed God and history on their side. It is one of the terrible ironies of history that the same Bible which accepts no distinction between races in the body of Christ (Colossians 3:11), has been cited by whites to justify the evil of apartheid. It is perhaps fitting that Woods escapes from the South Africa disguised as a priest and is driven across the frontier by a postman called Moses who is unaware he is parting the Red Sea for a fugitive.

As change gathers pace in South Africa, only time will tell what part people like Steve Biko and Donald Woods played in the future of that country. The American theologian Richard Neuhaus writes, "The debate about South Africa is in many ways a debate about the future of our life together on this small earth."[2] If so, *Cry Freedom* is an important film which captures both the infinite capacity for good and evil in humanity. In the end, it suggests, history will be decided by those who are willing to die for the truth, not those who do the killing. Those who look on Golgotha as the turning point in history would no doubt agree.

Mississippi Burning (1988)

"Hatred isn't something you're born with it, it gets taught. . . . The church tells you that Genesis says blacks are inferior. You go to school and you're taught hate. You grow up with it. You marry it."

The speech could well be made in South Africa, but this is the state of Mississippi, U.S.A., in the 1960s. Segregation is a way of life—blacks have separate eating areas, water fountains marked "Colored" and the burning crosses of the Ku Klux Klan to remind them what will happen should they try to upset the status quo.

Alan Parker's film takes its starting point from the murder of three civil rights workers in Mississippi in 1964. The three (two Jewish and one black) had been sent to organize a voter registration drive They were arrested on a minor offense, to be released only when the local Klan had met to arrange their murder. The murder is recorded history but around the known facts Parker weaves a compelling fiction about two FBI agents sent to investigate the case. Ward (William Dafoe), an idealistic "Kennedy boy," is teamed with Anderson (Gene Hackman), an easygoing pragmatic Southerner. From the start the combination smolders with friction and the personal differences between the two agents lend an added edge to the war between black and white that springs up around them. Ward, in charge of the investigation, is partly responsible for the way things get out of hand. By bringing in hundreds of FBI men he attracts the press circus who fuel with publicity the dormant hatred between the two communities.

Only when there is virtual civil war does Ward agree to Anderson's pragmatic, often brutal approach ("These people crawled out of the sewer, maybe the gutter's where we ought to be"). By kidnapping and terrorizing suspected members of the Klan, Anderson finally gets results. In view of the Klan's naked prejudice and gang murder it is hard not to cheer when Hackman beats up a Klan member in the local barber's. Nevertheless it is a hollow victory—if justice can only be brought about by fear and brutality, is the FBI any better than the South African police in *Cry Freedom?* Parker seems to condemn Ward's idealistic naiveté while backing Anderson's "means justifies the end" approach.

Mississippi Burning has also been criticized for presenting a misleading view of history. Parker has defended the film as a fiction based loosely on a framework of the real events of the 1960s. But is he justified in handling history in this way? Attenborough's film sticks closely to the events as seen by Donald Woods. The characters of Ward and Anderson, in contrast, are fictional creations, and critics have protested that the influence of the civil rights movement in the South is given little attention in the film.

Is This True?

Blacks appear mainly as victims, fleeing from burning homes or ambushed by Klan members after a church service. In the one point in the film where we see black leaders interviewed, their voices are not actually heard. What Parker actually gives us is history from a white point of view, with FBI men as the heroes. In fairness it must be said that whites come out of it pretty badly—not only in the smug prejudice of the townsfolk but in the failure of the imported northerners to understand the Southern culture they are dealing with.

Alan Parker, like all directors who turn to history for material, has narrowed his focus onto certain issues. In this case it is to examine hatred at close quarters, and it is the racism of the Ku Klux Klan rather than the courage of the black Americans that gives the film its focus. True, the dignity and faith of black gospel music is used throughout as a moving soundtrack, but it is often only to heighten the emotional impact of the lynch mob scenes of hanging and burning.

The local members of the Klan are shown as ordinary men bred on fear and hatred from an early age. At a Klan rally the camera picks out faces of children, terrified by scare-stories, who will convert their fear into hate in the next generation. After the murderers are tried and sentenced the body of a non-Klan member is found swinging from a noose he has made for himself. "He was guilty," Ward comments, "anyone is guilty who watches this happen—maybe we all are." If the film has a message it is that no one has clean hands, from the Klan killers to the callous townsfolk and blundering FBI.

Whatever its failings to do history justice, *Mississippi Burning* is a searing indictment of what happens when hatred is passed on from generation to generation in a community. Parker's film refuses to take the easy option of dismissing the Ku Klux Klan as crackpot fanatics in fancy dress. By opening up the festering evil lying just below the surface of small-town Mississippi he shows us the capacity for self-preservation and hatred that is within each of us. Prejudice in the full flower of racial murder is an ugly thing, but it begins with the small seed of considering anyone inferior. History is littered with the corpses of Jews, blacks, Catholics and Protestants who have been "inferior." Unless we uphold the worth and dignity of *every* human being as made in God's image there will always be the victims of inferiority.

The Last Emperor (1987)

If ever there was an epic historical film it is Bernardo Bertolucci's Oscar-laden masterpiece, *The Last Emperor*. Its story traces the history of modern China through the eyes of Pu-Yi, the last emperor of the Qing Dynasty. As Pu-Yi grows up in the bizarre world of the Forbidden City, history passes through the era of the warlords to the Second World War, the Japanese invasion and finally to the creation of the People's Republic of China.

That Bertolucci manages to make a coherent, let alone magnificent, film on such a broad canvas is a tribute to his skill. He does it by charting the changes in history by their effect on Pu-Yi. At the beginning we see a bewildered child staring at ranks of servants who bow to him as "the Lord of ten thousand years." By the end Pu-Yi himself is lost in a sea of grey uniformed citizens on bicycles. On one level the film is a rise-and-fall story on a grand scale, but on a deeper level it traces Pu-Yi's development as a human being, asking searching questions about the meaning of power, freedom and the role of the individual in history. Pu-Yi's early lessons in power are that the emperor is a god who can command anything he wishes. To prove his authority to his brother as a boy, he forces a servant to drink a bowl of ink. But the emperor's power is illusory—it exists only within the ancient world of the Forbidden City. When Pu-Yi attempts to go beyond its walls his own guards close the gate on him. As his Scottish tutor (Peter O'Toole) remarks, "The emperor has been a prisoner in his own palace since he was crowned."

History is often seen as people's struggle for power, but Bertolucci's film shows how power, can make a prisoner of those who possess it. Even presidents and royalty of the "free West" cannot go out for a walk whenever they feel like it. Throughout *The Last Emperor* Pu-Yi's cry "Open the door!" returns as a haunting refrain. His life is a continual struggle to escape, but like many people he mistakenly imagines that power will deliver the key to freedom.

When a warlord takes over, the emperor, now an adult, finally gets his wish to leave the Forbidden City. He lives the life of a Western playboy, seeking in the music and decadence of the West the freedom denied in his childhood. When the Japanese install him as the puppet emperor of Manchuria he realizes too late that he has only succeeded in trading one captivity for another. With Pu-Yi as a useful figurehead the Japanese proceed to bomb Pearl Harbor, experiment with chemical warfare on the Chinese and spread opium addiction to finance the war.

Dignity and Identity

The film tells the emperor's story in flashback, beginning in 1950 where Pu-Yi is a prisoner of the People's Republic. The prison governor tells him, "Men are born good. The only way to change is to discover the truth and look at it in the face." Pu-Yi, however, is neither willing to accept his responsibility for the past or change the present. He insists he was kidnapped by the Japanese, while still treating his cellmates as servants who must lace his boots for him. Before he can find any freedom Pu-Yi must discover the truth that each person is responsible for his or her own actions (Galatians 6:7).

There is a telling scene in the film where the emperor's consort leaves in the pouring rain and refuses an umbrella offered by a servant. It is a trivial gesture but one which expresses her individual freedom of choice. The emperor, by contrast, is always attended by a servant with an umbrella or coat—symbols of the way he is chaperoned through life. Without choice we have no meaning. History is made up of the choices we make (which Christians believe will one day come under God's judgment [Hebrews 9:27; Romans 2:16]). For Pu-Yi, then, tying his own bootlaces is the first step to admitting he must bear responsibility for his own choices, including his part in the Japanese crimes in China.

The film ends with the former emperor amid the sea of bicycles, now apparently a model Communist. But Bertolucci saves a twist in the tale until the last. Pu-Yi sees the former governor of his prison led as a prisoner in a revolutionary procession. Where the royal yellow of the emperor dominated Pu-Yi's childhoode now the red flag of Mao Tse-Tung billows against the sky.

Bertolucci calls the meaning of history into question with this last image. Is history nothing more than a change of names? A new emperor with a new flag and a different ideology swapped for the old? In this light the leaders of one revolution are simply the prisoners of the next—and the truth of this can be seen in many chapters of history. Power and politics are fickle masters, promising the world and often delivering only despair and disillusion.

Pu-Yi is in one sense the prisoner of history, never the master of his own fate but a victim of revolutions, from the warlords to Chairman Mao's Communism. Yet the film ends on an optimistic note with the former emperor returning to the Forbidden City and freeing his pet cricket from its prison under the throne. Despite the whims of history, Pu-Yi has finally gained the freedom that each of us possesses—to make meaningful choices and live in the world, accepting our responsibility for what we do.

A World View

In the three films we've considered, none of the characters escape the restraints of history. The sins of the fathers are visited on the sons who inherit the apartheid systems in South Africa and the American South, while Pu-Yi is born into a dynasty that is already dying. Henry Ford's view that "history is bunk" may be popular today, but it is not found in these films or in the Bible where God's dealings with the Jewish nation are constantly recounted to teach succeeding generations (Psalm 105; Hebrews 11).

Yet in their different ways each film depicts history as turning on the question of human choice. The choice to speak out about the evil of apartheid or remain silent, the choice to accept the prejudice of previous generations or fight it, the choice to become a captive to power or discover the freedom of accepting individual responsibility.

This reflects the paradox of history in the Christian world view. History is in the will of God, yet each of us has a choice that will affect our own destinies and the lives of others. As James Sire has expressed it, "History is not meaningless. Rather history is teleological, going somewhere, directed towards a known end. The God who knows the end from the beginning is aware of and sovereign over all human action."[3]

8
SAINTS AND SINNERS

In *Star Trek 5: The Final Frontier,* Captain Kirk and friends reach the end of the ultimate quest and come face to face with God. God appears in a Stonehenge-style temple; his eyes blaze, he has a long white beard and his voice thunders like an awakening volcano.

The character was so clichéd that, when I saw the film, most of the audience laughed out loud. Even Cecil B. DeMille would have fired this God for ham-acting. The makers of *Star Trek,* aware of the problem, added a twist where the Old Testament vision turned out to be nothing but an intergalactic con man.

The sequence perhaps explains why God gets such a raw deal in the cinema. In our skeptical age it is difficult to find a credible way of representing God. It is fine to have the Devil appearing out of a dry-ice smoke as a horned monster or drooling dog, but this fits comfortably in the horror genre. In the past God has been presented in terms of a heavenly light or a burning fire—both biblical images (Acts 9:3; Exodus 13:21)—but directors in the post De Mille era have shied away even from this. The only way of confronting the difficulty has been to call up the cliché of the old man in the sky through comedies like *Oh God!* where we get a very human George Burns in the divine role.

Faith on Film

Filmmakers cannot be blamed too much for their reluctance to cast God in the movies. After all, how do you portray someone who is immortal, all-powerful and all-seeing? The obvious way of showing an invisible God is to show his visible human followers—and this is where Christianity has more grounds for complaint against the film industry. Think of the men and women of faith you have encountered at the cinema. It shouldn't be hard; there aren't too many of them.

The examples we do find fit into a few categories. There are the religious maniacs—the missionary in *The Mosquito Coast* is a good example—the kind of person who finds it impossible to speak without spouting Bible quotations (usually about Hell and damnation) at every unfortunate he meets. There are the plausible hypocrites, often fallen priests with a weakness for sex, money or power (Robert De Niro in *True Confessions*). Finally, there are the simple country folk (the black churches in *The Color Purple* and *Mississippi Burning* or the Amish in *The Witness*). Although those in the last category are treated sympathetically, it is often their music and traditions that get Hollywood's attention rather than their real faith.

Films that include people of faith are rare—not one of the top twenty UK box office successes of the 1980s does so. Films that treat faith seriously, allowing the believers more than a two-dimensional personality are even rarer. Give cinema its due though; every now and then a diamond emerges from the mine which is worth waiting for. This chapter considers three of the films that break the stereotypes of religious belief in film. What do they tell us about the nature of faith and the struggle to maintain it in a hostile world?

Chariots of Fire (1982)

David Puttnam came across the idea for *Chariots of Fire* while reading a history of the Olympic games, during a bout of influenza. It took two years to find financial backing—nobody thought a film about British athletes in the 1928 Olympics would have any box office appeal. In fact, it is the strength of the two faiths underpinning the characters of Liddell and Abrahams that gives the film its inspiration. Churches all over Britain and America were suddenly recommending their members—often for the first time—to go to the cinema.

Puttnam's film is devoid of blockbuster ingredients. There is no special effects wizardry, no thrills-a-minute plot and no evil villain to be defeated. Instead the film, sustained throughout by Vangelis' score, taps strong emotions in its audience. From the opening shot of athletes striding through the surf we are put back in touch with forgotten values: the pursuit of excellence, team loyalty, love of country and honoring God.

Chariots of Fire is more than a nostalgic anthem to old virtues, though. It explores and opposes different creeds.

Abrahams and Liddell have differing goals in their pursuit
of honor. For Abrahams running is "a compulsion, a weapon
against being Jewish." His honor is the honor of the individual, fighting for respect and acceptance from a world that
sneers at his race. Liddell, by contrast, runs for his God—
"When I run I feel his pleasure . . . to win is to honor him."
A third creed opposes both of them—the creed of national
pride represented in the film by the Masters of Cambridge
and the British aristocracy which tries to persuade Liddell
to run against his principles.

Each view articulates a different faith. Where Abrahams
is running against prejudice, Liddell is running *for* the glory
of his Creator. It is the film's success in portraying "muscu-
lar Christianity" in a positive light that is so unusual. Why
does *Chariots* succeed where so many Christian films have
failed?

Liddell's faith is firstly an integration of the spiritual and
the physical. He understands that running cannot be sepa-
rated from living the life of faith. "You can praise God by
peeling a spud if you do it to perfection," as one character
observes.

Where some Christians have made the mistake of confusing mediocrity with modesty, Liddell longs for perfection
because he has been created in the image of a perfect God
(Matthew 5:48). Christians and nonbelievers alike can identify with the dedicated pursuit of excellence but in Liddell it
is purged of the dross of personal glorification.

Plaster Saints

The danger Puttnam must have been aware of, is to make
Liddell into a plaster saint. Although there is undoubtedly a

touch of the hero image, Liddell is never smugly pious. "The Sabbath's not the day for football," he tells a boy, but immediately arranges a game for the next morning. Whether running in braces and boots or finding time to sign an autograph after a mission service, Liddell possesses the common touch of a man who sees God in every human face. It is perhaps Christians' own fault that they are often portrayed as those who criticize from the sidelines; Liddell is an example of faith with its sleeves rolled up and in the middle of the action.

There is always a cost involved in faith, and *Chariots of Fire* does not attempt to gloss over the fact. For Liddell there is the pressure of his sister who feels he is neglecting the Mission work for his "secular" interest in running. The cost is borne by her too when Eric asks her to manage the Mission until after the games. Even harder is Liddell's decision not to run in the heats that take place on a Sunday. It is easily forgotten that Liddell's refusal to break what he believed to be God's law could have cost him a gold medal and everything he had sacrificed to take part in the Olympics. The pressure to take the pragmatic view reaches breaking point when Liddell is called before his future king in a last appeal to his patriotism. Liddell does not snap, but the film illustrates how faith doesn't always follow clearly marked paths. There are times Christians seem to follow God's leading into a cul-de-sac, and then faith's ultimate test is not to turn back.

When Christians appear on the big screen they tend to be secondary characters. By choosing Eric Liddell as one of the two central figures in *Chariots of Fire* Puttnam gives us a chance to see faith in close-up. In a film which is about old-fashioned heroes there is sometimes a tendency to idealize the characters. Liddell, for example, never really loses his temper or displays any doubts about his faith. Nevertheless, he is more than a two-dimensional character speaking religious clichés. Ian Charleson's portrayal is of a human being struggling to apply his beliefs against pressures few would be able to withstand. As a result, when Liddell crosses the line it is a victory that touches something inside an audience, a victory for perfection achieved through endeavor, honesty and a compelling faith.

"Where does the power come from to complete the race? It comes from within," preaches Liddell. As in the New Testament, the race is used as a frequent metaphor for life in the film (1 Corinthians 9:24; 2 Timothy 4:7). *Chariots of Fire* reminds us that it matters how we run. Compromise may be the language of modern politics and modern living, but it isn't the language of faith.

The Mission (1986)

If *Chariots of Fire* is a film about the triumph of faith over compromise, Roland Joffe's film *The Mission* paints a graphic picture of what happens when compromise corrupts individuals, nations and the church itself.

It is the 1750s. A political power game is developing in South America between Spain, Portugal and the pope. Portugal wishes to extend its lucrative slave trade into territory formerly belonging to Spain. The obstacle to this is the Jesuit missions which protect the Guarani Indians from slavery in their native territory. Portugal threatens to expel the Jesuit movement from its own country, and the pope is forced to send in his emissary to resolve the situation.

Caught up as pawns in the game are the Guarani and two

Jesuit priests, Father Gabriel (Jeremy Irons) and Rodrigo
Mendoza (Robert De Niro). Mendoza is a former slave trader
himself, brought to faith through the anguish of having
killed his own brother in a duel. Gabriel is the priest who
brings the gospel to the Guarani through music. For both
men the crisis of faith comes when the Portuguese come to
take the missions by force.

The central question is an age-old one for Christians. Is it
right to oppose the state when it acts unjustly? Is force ever
justified in resisting evil? The dilemma has not gone away in
our century; Christians in the Eastern bloc, South America
and South Africa have all had to face the issues Joffe raises
in *The Mission.*

The conclusions reached by Gabriel and Mendoza represent the two poles of opinion. Mendoza, faced with the destruction of the people he has adopted for his own, returns
to the power of the sword and organizes the Guarani to
defend themselves. Gabriel, on the other hand, chooses the
way of the cross. While the Portuguese attack, he holds
communion, confronting evil with the sacrifice of Christ's
body and blood. "If might makes right, then there is no room
for love in this world," he explains to Mendoza before the
conflict.

What's Not Said
The film avoids simplistic answers. Since the church has
betrayed the Indians into the hands of slave traders, isn't
Mendoza right to try and defend their cause? Gabriel's pac-
ifism can easily be seen as an empty gesture. On the other
hand Mendoza only succeeds in adding to the bloodshed—if
he had won the battle, could the missions be reborn through

the power of the sword? He dies witnessing a last vision of Father Gabriel advancing to greet death with the cross held high and flames consuming the surrounding village. The long final scene is ambiguous in meaning—are we seeing a pointless massacre of innocents or the martyrdom of saints embracing heaven as their ranks are shot down?

The film itself offers no hint of eternity for those who have died. The pope's emissary interprets the events for their significance to the living, "Your priests are dead and I am alive. But in truth it is I who am dead and they who live, for as always the spirit of the dead will survive in the memory of the living." In this respect *The Mission*'s picture is incomplete. If death is truly the end of those who lay down their lives following Christ, then evil has the last laugh. The Christian belief in eternity is crucial to belief in a God of justice who will right all wrongs committed on this earth (Romans 2:6-8).

The God of Power

The real victims of the film are the Guarani themselves. The pope's emissary cannot help wondering if they would have been happier if none of the Europeans had ever come to them. It is the age-old misgiving about missionary work. The Indians are idealized as noble savages, innocent in their nakedness, natural in their pleasures and gifted in music. But along with the gospel, the Europeans bring the taint of corruption with them. Spain and Portugal build their empires on land littered with corpses, and the Catholic Church turns a blind eye in the interests of self-preservation. "We must work in the world, the world is thus," shrugs the Portuguese representative. "No," replies the emissary, "thus have we made it, thus have I made it."

The harrowing final scene where the Guarani are slaughtered, leaves us feeling that they would indeed have been better off left in peace by both the soldiers and the Jesuits. Yet this is where the film is unsatisfactory in exploring the faith of the Guarani. In the Christian vision, death cannot have the last laugh on believers who have discovered a kingdom that exists beyond the grave (1 Corinthians 15:51-55). But the reality of faith among the Guarani is never explored because they aren't allowed to develop as characters. Instead what we get is an idealized vision of the Garden of Eden where the "noble savage" is taught to produce beautiful (Western) church music and to live in a community where all things are shared.

In the light of this, Father Gabriel's death may well be portrayed with the power of martyrdom, but the final taste the film leaves in the mouth is a bitter one. The massacre of the Guarani is a measure of the savagery to which "civilized men" will sink to serve their own greed. The spectacle of the church averting its eyes from the murder of a people it had come to save, warns how even believers can worship the god of power above the God of heaven.

A Cry in the Dark (1989)

From faith in the eighteenth century we return uncomfortably to the late twentieth century with Fred Schepisi's film, *A Cry in the Dark*. The film is a disturbing portrayal of real events that began in 1980 when a baby belonging to an Australian family was killed at Ayers Rock.

"The Dingo baby case" received huge publicity in Australia and around the world. Schepisi's film assumes the Chamberlain's innocence from the start and concentrates on the ordeal by trial and media that the family underwent when Lindy Chamberlain was accused of her child's murder.

The Chamberlain's story is one of faith in crisis, under the extreme pressure of a public trial. Michael Chamberlain is a Seventh-Day Adventist pastor, and his family share his beliefs. The story is played out against two backdrops—the vast specter of Ayers Rock, where the dingo steals the baby, and suburbia where the population of Australia devour the details of the case like flies buzzing around rotten meat.

Faith Under Pressure

The film doesn't dwell on the unorthodox aspects of Seventh-Day Adventism. It is a sympathetic portrait of ordinary people whose faith in the existence of a loving God is put to a severe test. The film begins and ends with the family happy and healthy in church, but in between the Chamberlains come to know how Job must have felt—abandoned by God and taunted by his neighbors.

The pastor is able to keep his faith airborne on autopilot when the baby first disappears. "I know that we'll see her again at the Resurrection," he tells the embarrassed crowd gathered to search. But it is his wife, Lindy, who proves the stronger in both her faith and her character. Michael passes from grief through anger to doubt and despair, "Prayer? What good is prayer? Hell can't be worse than this." Ironically, this makes him the more sympathetic character in the film's terms. Meryl Streep's characterization of Lindy is of an unyielding, outspoken woman with "a face that would turn milk sour." She stubbornly refuses to conform to the stereotypical heroine we can identify with. Learning the lesson that the press will exploit her feelings, she draws into herself, reading her Bible in private while presenting a strong, curt exterior. In the end this proves her downfall as neither the public nor the courts can accept that this is not the behavior of a murderer.

Prejudice runs through the film from the first obscenity of a truck driver passing the Adventists outside the church on their Sabbath. As one critic says, "Witch hunts tend to reveal the fears of nations and Australians appear to distrust Seventh-Day Adventists and uncompromising women in equal measures."[1] The Chamberlains are victimized both for their beliefs and for not showing their emotions in public. It is easy for those within the church to forget just how alien their ways appear to those outside. What appears a strong testament of faith to some is taken by others as evidence of a callous, even sinister nature.

Triumph or Failure?

A Cry in the Dark points the finger at other culprits besides the dingo. Both the media and the public are held responsible for the injustice the Chamberlains suffer. The press smell a good human-interest story at the start and then provoke the witch hunt by printing wild rumors about the Chamberlains belonging to a religious cult practicing child sacrifice. As one of the grandparents remarks, "A lie goes round the world while truth is still putting its boots on." In this case, the rumors and hearsay preoccupy most of Australia over its breakfast for the eight years that the controversy lasts. Ayers Rock and the dingo hold a special place in the great Australian outdoors, and most of Lindy's suburban judges have no problem in siding with them against a religious woman who hides her emotions.

The most moving scenes of the film show the strain telling in private on the Chamberlains' marriage. It is too easy to criticize Michael for his lack of faith in comparison to Lindy. None of us knows when a crisis will come along and shake our faith to prove that it relied less on God than on circumstances. But again cinema is better at showing the odds that are stacked against the believer than revealing much about faith itself. The film never resolves whether Lindy's survival has more to do with natural strength of character than depth of faith.

What *A Cry in the Dark* does suggest is that to rely on other people to get you through a crisis may not be enough—there are plenty of Job's comforters still about.

If the pictures of faith found in *Chariots of Fire, The Mission* and *A Cry in the Dark* have one thing in common it is their stress on the humanity of those who believe. Liddell, Father Gabriel and Lindy Chamberlain are all a long way from the two-dimensional televangelists and silly vicars that too often serve as Christian stereotypes on the big screen. Faith is not credible unless it is shown to confront the same doubts, fears, griefs and joys that other men and women must go through. Christians should take note. We have sometimes been guilty of producing books and films whose heroes have perfect lives and butter-wouldn't-melt-in-their-mouth smiles. Faith's calling is to live in the "between times." No one promised an easy ride—but then easy rides don't make good films anyway. It's no coincidence that directors, from Cecil B. De Mille to Martin Scorcese, have returned continually to the life of Christ.

9
HOW TO BE A MOVIE CRITIC
THE GOOD, THE BAD AND THE UGLY

> **"There's one God for all creation," said one producer, "but there must be a separate God for the movies. How else can you explain their survival?"**

It's a good question. People have been predicting the demise of cinema since it first began. The invention of television was to see it off, then the invention of video, but business is still booming at the box office.

There are many possible explanations for the film renaissance of the last ten years. The success of the blockbuster, the rediscovery of the family film, the introduction of multiplex cinemas, the emergence of big-name directors like Spielberg may all have played a part. But if we accept the argument at the beginning of this book—that films are closest to dreams in the way they portray our deepest desires, hopes and fears—then their enduring nature is not surprising. However little the films themselves live up to our high expectations we are reluctant to abandon our dreams. Even if the last film we saw was mindless fluff, it doesn't stop us going back next time still hoping for the extraordinary, the sublime and the profound.

A small number of the films reviewed in the preceding pages justify our hopes—providing something more than a couple of hours of escapism from the daily grind. What about the films of the 1990s? What brave new worlds are promised by the films of the decade ahead?

Films in the 90s

Judging from 1990 the signs aren't too promising. We seem destined like Michael J. Fox to keep on going back to the future—and when we get there all that's showing are more sequels. "Hollywood is nothing if not creative," enthused *Flick* magazine in April 1990. "This year, we'll be treated to sequels for films we haven't thought about in years!" That meant Jack Nicholson back in *Chinatown,* and *Godfather 3,* Tom Cruise in *Days of Thunder (Top Gun* with cars) to say nothing of *Rocky 5, Robocop 2, A Nightmare on Elm Street 5, Star Trek 6* and James Bond *still* refusing to be pensioned off by the Secret Service.

Thankfully this isn't the whole story. There are always surprise packages that will come through, even given the caution of the Hollywood moguls. The best example of that in 1990 was *Dick Tracy.* Even if he did raid the past for his hero, Warren Beatty's film pushed back the boundaries of cinema in its cartoonesque use of color, set and rubber-faced villains. There are also still directors like Woody Allen around, whose nineteenth film, *Crimes and Misdemeanors,* continued to ask serious questions about life and death under the surface of comedy. Films that capture our imaginations, disturb us or bring us face to face with life's mysteries, leave their images in the mind long after the thrill-formula films have faded away.

Evaluating Movies

Of course, it can be objected that this is a matter of opinion. You may find Woody Allen films self-obsessed and unfunny (people tend to love them or hate them). You may have thought *Days of Thunder* was a brilliant action film that got underneath the skin of the macho world of stock car racing. One person's meat is another's poison, as anyone can discover by going to see a film on a friend's recommendation!

What is a good or a bad film sounds like an unanswerable question. But for Christians, it is more important than it may at first sound. The Bible warns, "In your thinking be adults" (1 Corinthians 14:20). It is advice we should bear in mind when watching a film or video. Adults can enjoy entertainment as much as children but they should also be fully aware of what they're watching.

As Christians there are two key questions we should apply to any film we watch: *Is it good* and *is it true?* To understand what is meant by this we can break the questions down into smaller parts:

Is it Good?

1. *Is it original?*

There are really no new stories, but is the film just a tired reworking of clichéd situations or are there fresh, imaginative and inventive contributions from the director and others involved?

2. *Is it satisfying?*
Does it answer the questions it has raised, deliver its promises or settle for easy and simplistic solutions?—e.g., the big explosion or the happily-ever-after ending.

3. *Are they believable characters?*
If they are meant to be realistic, do they talk like real people? Do they behave true to their character or just obey the plot? Do they develop as the film progresses or remain two-dimensional?

4. *Does it engage us?*
Does the film capture our imagination from the start and unfold seamlessly? Or is it patched together, uneven in pace and confusing to follow?

Is it True?

A film can be great entertainment and still have a false message. In fact these are the films we need to be most aware of.

1. *What is its theme?*
As we've said, even Rambo films carry a message—"Tough guys win." Good films may explore two or three underlying themes. Once we identify what they are, its easier to decide if we can go along with the film's point of view. If you look back over the chapters of this book you'll find some of the themes that have emerged in recent popular films.

One way of evaluating the truth of a film is to look at its answers to specific questions. From a Christian viewpoint, key questions are:

2. *What exists?*
According to the film what is reality? Is it the material world or is there also a spiritual or supernatural dimension?

3. *What is the key to happiness?*
Is it portrayed as money, sexual love, power, status or something that always eludes us?
4. *What's right and wrong?*
Are there any moral absolutes, is it up to the individual, or is coming out on top all that counts?

Be a Film Critic
It bears repeating that the object of thinking about these sort of issues isn't to stop Christians from enjoying films. Far from it—the purpose is to help us to enjoy films more! By being your own film critic you can discover a lot more in a film. As Bob Bittner says, "Watching films critically can help you see anew the world that Christ died for. To let a film wash thrillingly over you and then allow it to evaporate as you step into daylight is to relinquish what films—both good and bad—are saying, 'I am a mirror of all the world.' "[1]

Trends and Patterns
This book has adopted the style of case studies on popular films to try to discover some of the themes and messages that are under the surface. We have looked at categories from space films to romances, from heroes to horror flicks.

It would be incomplete to end the book without asking what has been discovered from the exercise. Do any trends emerge from a survey of films from the late 1970s up to the present? If so, what do they tell us about the preoccupations of Western society as the twentieth century draws to a close?

Any attempt to draw conclusions from such a wide variety of films will be bound to make generalizations. But given this pitfall, I would single out the common feature of the films we've looked at as the way they reflect a search for answers. Where post-war films were still sure of their moral framework and 60s films were determined to break down that framework, the films of our age have been unsure of their direction—like luxury cruisers that are adrift from their moorings. No one is quite sure where we are heading and who is plotting the course. All that is certain is that the technical wizardry of modern cinema means that we'll always travel in style.

The search for answers evident in modern cinema could be described on three levels: a search for the extraordinary, a search for identity and a search for a savior-hero.

Search for the Extraordinary

When people say they want a film to take them out of themselves, they mean literally that. The magic lantern of the big screen can transport them out of their everyday lives and into the place of extraordinary people in exciting situations. More than ever, this is attractive to our generation. Modern society tells us there is no God, no ultimate purpose to living and no future beyond the grave. "We have a bleak, shallow rationalism that offers stones instead of bread to the emotional and spiritual hungers of the world. The logical result is an insatiable hunger for anything extraordinary."[2]

This craving can be seen in everything from the insatiable interest in the private lives of royalty to performing pets on TV shows. In the cinema it is reflected in films which include the gross, the exotic and the supernatural. The gross can be found in a recent burst of films which exalted bad taste into an art form. Whether comedy, horror or both, these films can usually be identified by scenes of dripping blood, gratuitous sex and anal humor. The sole imaginative idea is to shock an audience. In reality slob cinema like this is as bankrupt of imagination as the after-dinner speaker who forgets his words and resorts to belching loudly.

The taste for the exotic has always been around in the big-budget location film. Here the real star is the scenery. Recently India and Africa have been the fashionable choice *(Out of Africa, A Passage to India, Mountains of the Moon* and so on). More interesting are the supernatural films which hunt for the extraordinary beyond the material world. Steven Spielberg's *Always* (1990) is typical of the genre in bringing its hero back from the dead as a spirit, only to watch his former girlfriend fall for another fighter pilot. The majority of the films raid the supernatural world only to provide material for plots which are firmly earthbound. Cinema promises us the extraordinary but often only pulls another rabbit out of the hat.

Nevertheless, the hunger for the extraordinary in films is as insatiable as ever, suggesting that however much we say that the physical world is all there is, something in us deeply desires to be wrong.

A Search for Identity

Knowledge is not a problem at the end of the twentieth century. At the touch of a computer keyboard we can summon all the facts we need to know. Television keeps us informed of events on the other side of the world as they happen. If a war breaks out in South America we know within hours. But that doesn't help us to understand what is going on. For all the detailed information we can amass, we are less confident of the meaning of events than our ancestors. We are like characters trapped in a Spielberg film where dolls, train sets and pizzas are coming to life all around us but nobody explains what is happening or why.

Many contemporary films, especially sci-fi films, reflect this longing for a sense of meaning outside of ourselves. Since our God-framework (we have a personal Creator and are created for God's pleasure) has been taken away, we are forced to dream up our own meaning. The *Star Trek* series is a perfect example. The crew of the *Enterprise* travel through space to other worlds only to be reminded that humanity is its own meaning. There is no higher reality than the finer instincts within us. No one questions too much where these instincts come from. The *Enterprise* may go in search of God *(Star Trek 5)* but it always comes back to Captain James T. Kirk.

As many commentators have observed, the media has become the new priesthood of our secular society. In the place of moral absolutes, a purpose for living and a future hope, they have nothing to offer but more information and the magic of their art. As early as 1979 a *Newsweek* journalist wrote, "Films like *Close Encounter of the Third Kind, Superman* and even *Star Wars* have become cheap substitutes for the great myths and rituals of belief, hope and redemption that cultures used to shape before mass secular society took over."[3]

Search for a Savior-Hero

Our search for meaning can be seen most clearly in the enduring appeal of heroes within cinema. John Calvin once described life as a permanent factory of idols. Possibly our century's worship of matinee idols would not have surprised him. Film stars hold a sacred place in our society that is only rivaled by the stars of rock music. Really big stars like Madonna soon graduate to the silver screen.

Screen heroes, as we discussed in chapter three, come in different shapes and forms, but the most popular often have a savior dimension to them. By this I mean their job is to stand between us and disaster, one man rescuing the human race. Gotham City (read New York) is threatened by the Joker's greed—only Batman can save it. A hoodlum crime wave holds justice to ransom—call Dick Tracy. Planet earth is threatened by a series of cosmic villains—send for Superman. (In case we're in any doubt his father, Jor-El, spells out the messianic mission for us, "They only need the light to show them the way. For this reason, and this reason only, I have sent you my only son.")

Superman and Batman combine our craving for the fantastic with our need for a savior-hero. Their flowing capes and swimming trunks mark them as different from the rest of the race (in real life they would get arrested). They are fantasy heroes whom we can laugh at and cheer at the same time because we know their exploits have little to do with real life.

Heroes like James Bond and Indiana Jones, in contrast, are very much one of us. They have no powers beyond their human resources of quick thinking, gutsiness and courage. Nevertheless the "savior of the human race" role is thrust upon them too. If nuclear weapons fall into the hands of an evil genius only one man, Bond, can save the earth from destruction. Similarly, in the Indiana films our hero is called upon to singlehandedly thwart Nazi imperialism or (on an off day) rescue an entire tribe from occult domination.

The golden rule is that heroes never die. While we know it is ridiculous for Bond to continuously survive while agents fall like flies around him, and for Jones always to escape in the nick of time, we are more than willing to suspend our disbelief. Our heroes can be human but must remain immortal. A savior figure who dies would be of no use at all—unless of course he returned to life like E.T.

Still Searching

By now you may suspect that we are all set for the conclusion that what every film is actually looking for is Jesus Christ. This, of course, is obviously not true. In most cases film companies and directors are looking to make entertaining films that pull in the crowds and earn a profit.

Nevertheless, what's interesting is that, while most of the films quoted here studiously avoid all mention of God, Jesus or even religion, they so often find themselves back at fundamental religious questions. The three strands we've identified in contemporary film reflect this. Our desire for the extraordinary is born out of a feeling that there must be more to life than the material world. Our search for identity involves looking for a meaning beyond ourselves. And, most obviously, our need for a savior-hero admits that Captain Kirk and the wonder of the human race is not enough. We are looking for something better than humanity.

On the surface of it, films in the 70s and 80s had little to do with Christianity, but a closer look suggests otherwise. Melissa Mathison's discovery—that she had closely paralleled the life of Christ in her screenplay for *E.T.*—shouldn't come as such a surprise. If films are our waking dreams then they will often show up humanity's highest ideals and deepest aspirations.

Notes

Chapter One: Under the Influence

[1]Roy E. Disney, interviewed in *Empire Magazine,* December 1989.

[2]Doug McClelland, *Starspeak: Hollywood on Everything* (Faber and Faber, 1987).

[3]John Ellis, *Visible Fictions* (Routledge and Kegan Paul, 1982).

[4]McClelland, *Starspeak.*

Chapter Two: To Boldly Go

[1]Mott, McAllister and Saunders, *Steven Spielberg* (Columbus Books, 1986).

[2]Robert Short, *The Gospel from Outer Space* (Fount, 1983).

[3]Jack Kroll, *Newsweek,* November 1977.

[4]Mott, McAllister and Saunders, *Spielberg.*

[5]C. G. Jung, "The UFO as Religious Symbol," quoted in Mott, McAllister and Saunders, *Spielberg.*

[6]Tom O'Brien, "Steven Spielberg's Suburban Animism—Very High Sci-Fi," *Commonweal,* August 1982.

[7]Robert Short, *Gospel from Outer Space* (Fount, 1983).

[8]Interview with George Lucas in *Chicago Sunday Times,* May 18, 1980.

[9]Carl Sagan, *Broca's Brain* (Ballantine Books, 1980).

Chapter Three: My Hero—So Macho

[1]Harvey Keitel, quoted in Doug McCllelland, *Starspeak: Hollywood on Everything* (Faber and Faber, 1987).

[2]Mott, McAllister and Saunders, *Steven Spielberg* (Columbus Books, 1986).

[3]Barbara L. Baker, It's a Boy's Life," quoted in Mott, McAllister and Saunders, *Spielberg.*

Chapter Four: Modern Love Stories

[1]Doug McCllelland, *Starspeak: Hollywood on Everything* (Faber and Faber, 1987).

[2]John Ellis, *Visible Fictions* (Routledge and Kegan Paul, 1982).

[3]Groucho Marx, quoted in McCllelland, *Starspeak.*

Chapter Five: Nightmares Are Fun

[1]Kim Newman, *Nightmare Movies* (Bloomsbury, 1988).

[2]David Thompson, *Overexposures: The Crisis in American Film-making,* quoted in Kim Newman, *Nightmare Movies.*

[3]Newman, *Nightmare Movies.*

[4]Ibid.

Chapter Seven: History in the Making

[1]Richard Attenborough, *Cry Freedom: A Pictorial Record* (Bodley Head, 1987).

[2]Richard J. Neuhaus, quoted in Michael Cassidy, *The Passing Summer* (London: Hodder and Stoughton, 1989).

[3]James W. Sire, *The Universe Next Door,* 2d ed. (Downers Grove, Ill.: InterVarsity Press, 1988).

Chapter Eight: Saints and Sinners

[1]Mark Cooper, *Empire Magazine,* December 1989.

Chapter Nine: How to Be a Movie Critic

[1]Bob Bittner, "Finding Gold on the Silver Screen," in *The Time of Your Life* (Leicester, England: Inter-Varsity Press, 1989).

[2]C. G. Jung, *Flying Saucers: A Modern Myth of Things Seen in the Skies* (Princeton, N.J.: Princeton University Press, 1978).

[3]From *Newsweek,* January 1, 1979, as quoted in Robert Short, *The Gospel from Outer Space* (Fount, 1983).

Index of Movies